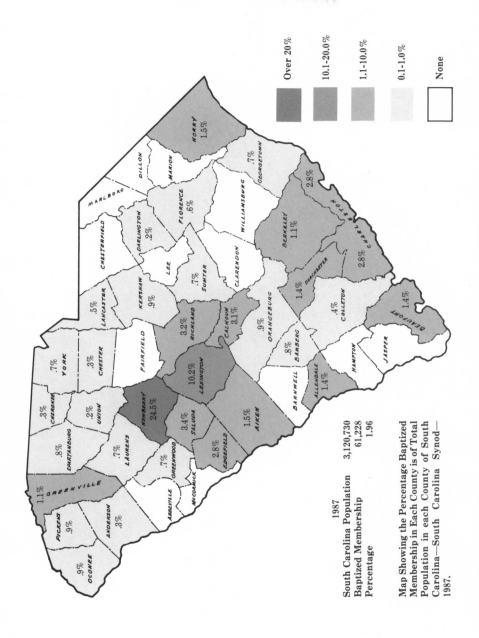

1987
South Carolina Population   3,120,730
Baptized Membership   61,228
Percentage   1.96

Map Showing the Percentage Baptized
Membership in Each County is of Total
Population in each County of South
Carolina—South Carolina Synod—
1987.

Over 20%
10.1-20.0%
1.1-10.0%
0.1-1.0%
None

A HISTORY
OF THE
LUTHERAN CHURCH
IN
SOUTH CAROLINA
1971-1987

SOUTH CAROLINA SYNOD
Lutheran Church in America

1003 Richland Street
P. O. Box 43
Columbia, South Carolina 29202

A HISTORY

OF THE

LUTHERAN CHURCH

IN

SOUTH CAROLINA

1971-1987

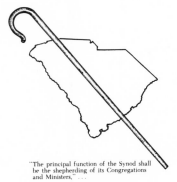

"The principal function of the Synod shall
be the shepherding of its Congregations
and Ministers," . . .

*—From the Constitution of the
South Carolina Synod of the
Lutheran Church in America,
1980.*

Published by
THE SOUTH CAROLINA SYNOD
OF THE
LUTHERAN CHURCH IN AMERICA

Prepared and Edited by
HISTORY OF SYNOD COMMISSION

1988

© *Copyright 1988 by*
The South Carolina Synod
of the
Lutheran Church in America

Library of Congress Catalog Card No. 88-61596
ISBN 0-934870-24-1

Printed by
THE R. L. BRYAN COMPANY
COLUMBIA, SOUTH CAROLINA
1988

Preface

As it became clearer and clearer that the Lutheran Church in America would be involved in a merger with other Lutheran bodies, the 1982 Convention, upon the recommendation of the bishop and the executive board, authorized the establishment of a History of Synod Commission and the funding for the writing and publication of such a history. This volume is to be a companion volume to *A History of the Lutheran Church in South Carolina*, 1971, which gives a detailed history of Lutheranism in South Carolina from the early years of the 1700's until its publication in 1971. This volume, therefore, begins at the point the 1971 volume concludes and ends with December 31, 1987, the effective date of the end of the Lutheran Church in America.

After a slow and difficult start that included the resignation of the first two chairpersons, the commission began its work in earnest in 1984. Biographical information was already being gathered from the pastors who had served in the synod since 1971, and work now needed to proceed on the congregational histories and the general work of the synod. The work of the commission was divided as follows:

Editor and Writer . . . . The Rev. James B. Park
Pastoral Biographies . . . . Miss Mary Boozer and
the Rev. James B. Park
Congregational Histories . The Rev. Russell B. Kleckley,
Mrs. Kathleen Fesperman, and
the Rev. Dr. Douglas Johnson
Committees and Synodical History . . Mrs. Virginia Aull
Institutions and Auxiliaries . . Miss Margaret Paysinger
Statistical Data . . . . The Rev. Dr. James S. Aull
Pictures and General
Counsel . . . . The Rev. Dr. Herman W. Cauble
Index and Research . The Rev. Dr. W. Richard Fritz, Sr.

In the narrative section, we have sought to describe the general work of the synod, the committees, auxiliaries, institutions, and agencies. Congregational histories have been written to reflect the scope of the ministry of each congregation since 1971. Statistical data for each congregation as of December 31, 1971, and December 31, 1987, is included in Appendix 3. Biographical data was gathered on all pastors who were at any time on the Roll of Ministers of the South Carolina Synod since 1971. Some of these were ordained by the synod and transferred to another synod for service; others came to this synod after retirement. In either case, specific places and dates of service outside the South Carolina Synod before or after their being a part of this synod have not been included. A listing of the Certified Lay Professionals as of December 31, 1987, along with some biographical information, has also been included.

We have also included in Appendix 6 corrections to the 1971 volume as they have been reported to us and verified. We hope that errors in this volume are few, but we do request that any noted be reported to the Editor or the synod office.

I am deeply indebted to all the pastors and lay persons who provided us with information for this volume. I am particularly indebted to the members of the Commission who provided their time and talents to the development of this volume, and to Bishop Cauble for his continued support and interest in our work. We also thank Mrs. Carolyn Huntley and Mr. Timothy Yount for their early leadership of this commission.

James B. Park,
Editor

Camden, S. C., 1988.

Contents

Contents—*continued*

Chapter One—The Synod

With over two hundred and fifty years of history as a foundation, the Lutheran Church in South Carolina moved into the 1970's and 80's as a part of the Lutheran Church in America, and continued the growth, both in congregations and ministry programs, that had characterized the earlier years. The most notable area of growth for the synod was in the Grand Strand area—along the beaches of South Carolina. Only one congregation had served that area since 1956, and the growth of the area, both in tourism and in permanent residents, brought the need for additional congregations. In 1975 and 1976, two congregations were organized along the Grand Strand, one at the south end, Shepherd of the Sea, Garden City in November, 1975,[1] and one at the north end, King of Glory, North Myrtle Beach in November, 1976.[2] These two congregations grew rapidly, and were joined in their service to the beach area by St. Peter, Pawleys Island in 1984[3] and Christ the Servant, Conway in 1986.[4] The Charleston area of the South Carolina coast had also experienced tremendous growth around its perimeters, and the development of new congregations in that area was also a key part of the Lutheran church's ministry during this time. Christ, Hilton Head was organized in 1973[5] to serve that new community and was soon joined by the congregations of Peace, Ladson (North Charleston) in 1974,[6] All Saints, Mt. Pleasant in 1975,[7] and A Mighty Fortress, Sangaree (Summerville) in 1981.[8] But growth was not limited to the coastal areas of the state. The Piedmont section experienced the development of two new congregations with Redeemer, Greer being organized in 1972[9] and St. Matthias, Easley, organized in 1974.[10] Cross and Crown expanded the ministry of the Lutheran church in the Florence area with its organization in 1981,[11] and Christus Victor was established in the new community of Harbison, northwest of Columbia in 1986.[12] In the summer of 1987, a new mission field was entered when a pastor/developer under call of the synod began work in the northeastern part of Columbia.

1

With support from the Division for Mission in North America of the LCA, Living Springs Lutheran Church began worship services on November 15, 1987. The worshipers look forward to their organization as a congregation of the Evangelical Lutheran Church in America.

Pastor Larry Bost worships at synod convention with sign language.

But the most distinctive new congregation for South Carolina Lutherans resulted from the development of the Ministry with the Deaf in Columbia in 1985.[13] Organized as a congregation, these Lutherans provide a special ministry for people with hearing disabilities and their families. They are led by a hearing-impaired pastor who not only ministers to their needs, but also extends his ministry to much of the hearing impaired community in Columbia, including those in hospitals and prisons. This congregation worships in the Chapel of St. Paul, Columbia. (See page 169.)

Interest in, and support for, the development of new Lutheran congregations was demonstrated by members of the South Carolina Synod throughout these years by their participation in several special projects.

The 1974 LCA Convention in Baltimore adopted the program of "Strength For Mission," and in 1976 the LCA Convention in Boston set the goal at $25 million for a campaign during 1977-78. Money from this campaign was used to strengthen this mission of the LCA in North America and overseas.[14] The South Carolina Synod pledged over $670,000 to this campaign, exceeding the LCA guideline for the synod. Mr. Arthur W. Sedler, a layman of the synod, served as director of the synodical campaign.[15]

A special Reformation Offering to be received in October 1984, was approved by the synod convention challenging

LCA President Robert J. Marshall (center) meets with "Strength For Mission" leaders, including Mr. Arthur Sedler (right), Director for South Carolina.

each congregation to make a gift amounting to at least $1.00 per confirmed member in addition to its regular benevolence offerings, to be divided equally between support for new LCA congregations and support for the LCA World Mission program.[16]

A second campaign, called "One in Mission," with payments to be made from July 1986-June 1989, was conducted throughout the LCA and the South Carolina Synod. The LCA goal of $36 million was earmarked for new mission congregation development ($30 million) and as a birth gift for the Evangelical Lutheran Church in America ($6 million). In the South Carolina Synod the goal was $1.4 million with $933,333 designated for the LCA goals, $311,111 for Newberry College, and $155,556 for Southern Seminary.[17] The Rev. Hugh E. Baumgartner served as general chairman. Again the synod exceeded its goal with pledges of over $1.7 million.[18]

Throughout all of these years, the primary purpose of the Lutheran Men of South Carolina has been the financial support of mission congregations through their Loan and Gift Funds. In the years of 1971 to 1987, nineteen different congregations received low interest loans of over $777,000 and twenty-six different mission congregations received gifts of over $233,000 (see page 62).

Upon the retirement of the Rev. Dr. Herman W. Cauble as Bishop of the South Carolina Synod, the Executive Board authorized the establishment of the Herman W. and Elizabeth Petrea Cauble Mission Trust Fund. Over $17,000 has been contributed to this fund in honor of Dr. and Mrs. Cauble (see page 6).

In addition to these special projects, the congregations of the synod have supported the development of mission congregations through special gifts made directly to them. All of these are evidence of the strong sense of mission in South Carolina.

But growth of the Lutheran church in South Carolina was not limited to the development of these new congregations. During the period 1972 to 1987, the baptized membership grew each year from 51,606 in 1972[19] to 61,282 in 1987, with 38,481 communing, contributing, confirmed members.[20]

Officers and Staff

Through these years, the synod continued to enjoy strong leadership from its elected officers, pastors, and laity. The Rev. Dr. Herman W. Cauble had been elected President of

Bishop Herman W. Cauble is flanked by Secretary James S. Aull (left), and Treasurer James B. Wessinger (right).

the synod in 1971, and the Rev. Paulwyn L. Boliek was elected to succeed Dr. Cauble as secretary of the synod.[21] With the Rev. Lloyd W. Mitcham, Jr. as the Executive Secretary of Christian Education, and Mr. James B. Wessinger as Treasurer, they provided the synod with the effective leadership that was needed to move through the 1970's. In 1979, Secretary Boliek resigned to become pastor of Resurrection, Augusta, Georgia, and the Rev. Dr. James S. Aull was elected Secretary of the Synod.[22] The office of president was changed by the convention of the LCA in 1980 to bishop.[23] In 1981, Mr. Wessinger retired as treasurer after

Treasurer Raymond S. Caughman.   *Assistant to the Bishop Robert L. Dasher.*

20 years of service. A scholarship at Newberry College was established in his honor, and over 500 people attended a dinner honoring Dr. Wessinger and Mrs. Carolyn Sanders, bookkeeper.[24] Mr. Raymond S. Caughman was elected treasurer by the synod convention in 1981.[25] Pastor Mitcham resigned as Executive Secretary of Christian Education and Youth Ministry in 1984 to accept a call in North Carolina. The executive board authorized a change in the title and responsibilities for this position, and in 1985, called the Rev. Robert L. Dasher as Assistant to the Bishop.[26]

Bishop Cauble receives a cross upon his retirement from the Rev. Guy C. Cruse, Chairman of the recognition committee.

The Rev. Dr. Herman W. Cauble retired as Bishop of the South Carolina Synod on December 31, 1987. A banquet in his honor was held at Newberry College on October 18, 1987 with about 400 in attendance. In addition to small, personal gifts to him and Mrs. Cauble, along with a Book of Letters from people throughout the synod, the Herman W. and Elizabeth Petrea Cauble Mission Fund was established to help new mission congregations in South Carolina.[27] The Rev. Dr. James S. Aull was elected to serve as the Bishop of the new South Carolina Synod of the Evangelical Lutheran Church in America.[28]

In addition to these people, the synod has been faithfully served by people working on the various committees and boards of the synod to develop the ministry programs and enhance the outreach and witness of the Lutheran church in South Carolina.

On November 23, 1983, the Rev. Dr. Karl W. Kinard, President Emeritus of the South Carolina Synod, died. He was only the second full-time president of the synod, having served from 1943 to 1971. Prior to that he had served as the secretary of the synod, 1935 to 1943, in a part-time position. His wife, Esther, had died in July 1983.[29]

January 14, 1974, marked the 150th anniversary of the organized Lutheran synod within the boundaries of South Carolina. In recognition of this anniversary, a special program of celebration was held on Sunday, January 13, at the Carolina Coliseum in Columbia. Over 8,000 people attended this service that included the Rev. Dr. Robert J. Marshall, President of the Lutheran Church in America, as the speaker, an afternoon concert before the service, and a spe-

150th Anniversary celebration at Carolina Coliseum.

cial anniversary hymn composed by Professor Gordon Beaver of the Lutheran Theological Southern Seminary. An historical pageant with Holy Communion was held at the Township Auditorium on Sunday, April 28, as the opening of the synod convention, with an anniversary reception following at St. Paul Lutheran Church. Music for this special service was provided by the seminary choir, a joint handbell choir, and the Airport High School Chorus. Ushers were from the youth of the synod, and the reception was provided by the Lutheran Church Women. A special thankoffering was received by the congregations of the synod on the sunday before Thanksgiving, 1974, in honor of the 150th anniversary and designated for the Loan Fund for mission congregations in South Carolina.[30]

For years, the synod had been operating with five districts. In 1975, after a study by the Committee of Deans, the synod convention approved a realignment that resulted in eight districts to be organized by not later than October 15, 1975.[31] The purpose of each district was to "assist in caring for and developing the church on its territory, to provide liaison between the synod and the congregations of the district, and to perform such other functions, . . . , as the synod may assign to it." [32] Each district met twice a year, elected a dean, secretary, and cabinet, which was composed of the clergy and lay representatives to the five operational committees of the synod. The deans of the districts served as a committee to review and act on the status of pastors "whose status is subject to reconsideration," represent the district at congregational and auxiliary events, and other tasks as were needed for the ministry of their districts.[33]

The business of the synod was transacted at an annual convention held in the spring of the year. For years these conventions were held at various congregations throughout the synod, but in 1982, the conventions were moved to Newberry College where they have been held since. In 1974, the convention authorized an additional lay delegate for every

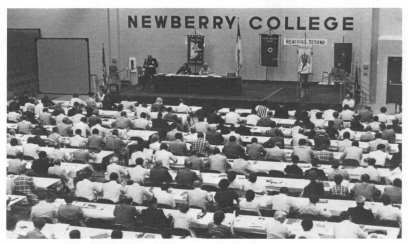

The synod in convention at Newberry College.

congregation with an active confirmed membership of over 250.[34] With the growth in the number of congregations and pastors, and the addition of these lay delegates, the synod soon outgrew the facilities of most congregations. Newberry College provided the synod with the necessary facilities for meetings, overnight accommodations, and meals. The time for these conventions was moved to a date after college commencement, and alternated between weekend and weekday conventions, with the various districts serving as hosts.

In 1973, the Church House at the corner of Richland and Park streets in Columbia was free of debt for the first time since its erection in 1958 and expansion in 1964. Here the offices of the bishop and other synod staff, the synodical film library, and other related offices are housed. In 1987, the building underwent a complete renovation at a cost of $100,000, paid for by a loan of $75,000, and synod reserves.[35]

Inclusive Ministry

Throughout these two decades, the synod experienced a growing awareness in the area of inclusive ministry—that is ministry with minorities, especially blacks and women. The executive board approved the idea of a mission congregation in the Eau Claire section of Columbia to serve the needs of those residents, particularly the blacks. In 1971, the Committee on American Missions, in cooperation with the Board of American Missions of the LCA, called the Rev. William Batterman, who carried on a short-lived mission in that area.[36]

In 1979, a Task Force on Minority Ministries was formed by the Social Ministry Committee of synod, and in 1985, it became an autonomous committee of synod.[37] The committee began its work by surveying and noting the positive changes throughout the synod in the area of racial inclusiveness. Beginning in 1980, it began work on an Equal Employment Opportunity Statement that was adopted by the synod convention in 1981. This statement calls for the executive board of synod to engage employees without regard to sex, race, or nationality, ethnic or religious background, except in instances in which preference should be

The Rev. Garey Green (right), newly ordained, and his sponsor, the Rev. Dermon A. Sox, Jr. (left).

given to members of Lutheran congregations. That convention also adopted a Statement on Racial Inclusiveness that commits the South Carolina Synod to "the elimination of all racial barriers and to the opening of the doors of all congregations to all people." [38] This statement was reaffirmed at the convention in 1984.[39] In 1982, a resolution was adopted calling for congregations to affirm the inclusiveness of its ministries to all the people of its communities.[40] In 1983, the first black person was ordained by the South Carolina Synod.[41]

As a result of the 1976 Convention action, the synod secretary was asked to compile and report statistics concerning the levels of participation by women in the leadership roles of congregations and the synod.[42] The Secretary reported increasing numbers of women in positions of responsibility in the church, but still far less proportionately than their membership numbers. This growth in women's inclusiveness is evidenced by the following: in 1972, of the 128 lay delegates to the South Carolina Synod Convention, 13 (10%) were women; in 1976, of 189 delegates, 42 (22%) were women; in 1972, of the 8 lay delegates from South Carolina to the LCA Convention, only 1 (12.5%) was a woman; in 1976, of the 8 lay delegates, 4 (50%) were women.[43]

Conventions of the synod adopted several resolutions dealing with issues before the people and the legislature of the state. Among them were 1982 Convention actions opposing the storage of nuclear waste from other states in South Carolina[44] and supporting the bilateral freeze on the development and deployment of nuclear weapons;[45] 1983 Convention action opposing any attempt to legalize gambling in South Carolina;[46] action expressing opposition to the sale of children in South Carolina by the 1984 Convention;[47] and the support of reform of the adoption laws of South Carolina by the convention of 1985.[48] The synod also adopted a resolution supporting significant minority representation in the South Carolina Senate;[49] and a resolution supporting the removal of the Confederate flag from the top of the State House was adopted in 1986.[50]

Ecumenism

Ecumenism was certainly an area of growth during the decades of the 70's and 80's. Most of this work was carried out through the Christian Action Council of South Carolina, of which the South Carolina Synod is a supporting member. The purpose of this Council has been to enhance the cooperative efforts among churches and individual Christians and to identify common concerns and to develop avenues for working together to translate those concerns into action. Legislative seminars and programs for new pastors in the state are but two of the Council's programs.[51] In 1971, the Council faced a financial crisis when the Internal Revenue Service ruled that it was not a "religious" agency, and must, therefore, pay taxes, although contributions to it were tax exempt as "educational charitable" deductions. An appeal of this ruling resulted in the overturning of the IRS ruling in 1972.[52] The 50th anniversary of the Council in 1983 showed that involvement by the South Carolina Synod began in 1952 with support steadily growing through the years. The relationship with the Lutheran Church was strengthened in 1983 when the council moved into rented quarters at Southern Seminary.[53] In 1985, the Rev. Dr. Howard McClain resigned as Executive Director after over 35 years of service. The Rev. Dr. Russell B. Norris became the Executive Minister in 1986, the first Lutheran to hold that position.[54] Eighteen church bodies, with more than 6,000 congregations and nearly 1.8 million Christians across South Carolina, support the work of the Council.

One of the biggest steps in ecumenism occurred in 1984 with the development of the Episcopal-Lutheran Dialogue. A statement endorsing this document and establishing procedures by which Lutherans and Episcopalians could share in the celebration of Holy Communion was adopted and signed by the Bishops of the Upper and Lower Diocese of the Episcopal Church and the Bishop of the South Carolina Lutheran Synod. A conference on this dialogue and document was held in Columbia, and since then a number of shared services of Holy Communion have been celebrated throughout the state.[55]

Episcopal Bishops William A. Beckham and C. FitzSimons Allison (left and right), and Bishop Cauble sign "Guidelines for the Joint Celebration of the Eucharist between Lutheran and Episcopal Churches in South Carolina."

In 1987, another ecumenical highlight was the visit of Pope John Paul II to Columbia. Although the synod was not officially involved in the preparations for this visit, four national Lutheran leaders attended a conference with other leaders of the Christian and Jewish churches in America and the Pope at the University of South Carolina. A number of Lutheran clergy and laity shared in the Christian prayer service that was held at Williams-Brice Stadium. The next day, Southern Seminary hosted a meeting of the Christian leaders who had come to Columbia to discuss further the road of ecumenism. Over 300 people attended the conference.

Midlands Lutheran Council

Because the Columbia metropolitan area, like many other cities, is undergoing enormous changes and is presenting an increasing challenge to our congregations to witness effectively, in August 1984, Bishop Cauble formed an Area Mission Study Committee to examine the community and how to enhance the ministry of the Lutheran church in, and around, the area. Years of hard, sophisticated work, with the assistance of the Rev. Boyce Whitener of the LCA's Division for Mission in North America, resulted in the publication of the *Midlands Area Mission Strategy, 1986-1996*, a proposed plan for ministry. Detailed data on the demographic composition of congregations and parishes provided concrete basis for planning. Also came a proposal that the area congregations, which have long cooperated informally, work together on a more formal basis as the Midlands Lutheran Council. To guide the new Council, the study committee drew up a Statement of Mission, Principles of Mission, and a set of goals toward enhancing the cooperative ministry of the Lutheran church in the community and with other denominations. The Midlands Lutheran Council first met in May 1987, at Ebenezer Church, Columbia. The Statement of Mission, Principles of Mission, and Goals were approved, and the Board of Directors with four clergy and eight lay members was elected. Representatives of the bishop, Newberry College, LTSS, Lutheran Social Services of Central South Carolina, the Lowman Home, and the LCA Division for Ministry in North America are also members of the board. The board met monthly in 1987 drawing up ideas for ways to serve the Lutheran church in the Columbia area. In late June 1987, the Council met again to advise the board on a variety of projects and proposals. With the Council's approval, the board has worked on promotion and publicity for the 1987 Reformation services and plans for the 1988 Reformation service; a survey of congregations to discover unique and common areas of ministry; long-range planning; and "professional leadership events" for pastors and other church leaders. Thirty-six area congregations are participating in the Midlands Lutheran Council.[56]

The South Carolina Lutheran

The Synod Executive Board elected the Rev. D. Murray Shull, Jr. as the "interim editor" of the *South Carolina Lutheran* on August 30, 1966. The subsequent convention of synod confirmed the appointment by electing him Editor and re-electing the Rev. G. B. Corley as Business Manager,[57] a position he had held since 1957. The new editor reported to the synod convention of 1968: "The position of editor . . . is a sobering responsibility. By the news printed or omitted is inferred what is relevant, or not relevant, to the life of the synod and its congregations." [58]

Editions during the first few years under Pastor Shull revealed only slight changes in the design, omission of the "Editorial," use of occasional guest editorials (usually from other church publications), and the addition of "The Worship Corner," a regular feature for about four years. In 1969, the number of pages was increased from eight to twelve in six of the eleven issues.

At the end of 1968, the subscriptions numbered 11,505, and for the next ten years there was a steady increase in the number of subscribers. By 1976, when the growth reached over 14,000, the Newberry Observer Company, which had printed and mailed the publication for forty years, found it necessary to request that another firm be engaged to do the work. Crown Printing Company of Greenville took over the printing function, with computer printed address labels supplied by Data Systems, Inc., also of Greenville, until Mr. Fred Lester of Newberry took over this function.

The changes brought on by the increased subscriptions evolved into an exciting transition in 1977 that offered expansion at a reasonable cost into the occasional use of color and art work, additional pages, coded labels, and printouts by congregations and districts. "It's been a year of extra work and rewards as we have grown in providing a quality publication to serve the people of the South Carolina Synod," reported Editor Shull.[59] At the end of 1977, the subscription list numbered 15,229, and only 34 out of 150 congregations were not on the Every Home Subscription Plan.

Funding of a synodical publication reflects many factors in its history. *The Lutheran Messenger*, the original predecessor periodical, "published monthly in the interests of the Evangelical Lutheran Synod of South Carolina," in 1922 distributed 5,000 free sample copies of its first issue among the congregations. The initial annual subscription price was fixed at fifty cents.[60] Synod records show that for just over twenty years there were three sources of income for *The South Carolina Lutheran*: subscriptions, synod (budgeted allocation), and the women's auxiliary of synod. The records show an annual contribution that ranged from $50.00 to $150.00 per year from the women from 1954 through 1975. In 1970, synod gave an additional allocation above the budgeted amount to underwrite increased costs, and in 1977, extra monies were authorized to finance the changeovers mentioned above. The 1982 Convention of synod adopted a budget for 1983 that doubled the funding for the *South Carolina Lutheran* from $6,000 to $12,000. Increased to $13,000 in 1984, the budget allocation dropped back to $12,000 in 1985 through 1987. Mounting postal costs during this period had a definite impact on publications of this type.

Subscription rates fall into two categories: a congregational (when every member home is included) and an individual subscription rate. In 1971, increasing costs forced a rate increase to $1.00 per year for the congregational plan, and $1.50 for the individual plan. By 1980, those rates had doubled; but the 1982 rates of $2.50 for the congregational plan, and $3.50 for the individual plan were still in effect in 1987.

Subscription numbers likewise reflect the acceptance and support of congregations and members. Peaking in 1978 at 15,286 (possibly in response to the addition of color, improved type styles, etc.), there was a period of leveling off until 1983 when the 15,000 mark was reached again with 130 churches on the congregational plan. At the end of 1987, there were 16,971 subscriptions with 132 on the congregational plan and 30 on the individual plan.[61] It took 32 years (1922-1954) to reach the initial goal of 3,000 subscriptions for the synodical publication,[62] and in the next 32 years, that number increased more than five times.

While the 1980's were years of increased support through increased funding by the synod and increased numbers of subscriptions, there were other indications of the success of the *South Carolina Lutheran*. Editor Shull reported to the 1982 Convention: "It has been a great year for the *South Carolina Lutheran*. We were the top winner among all Lutheran Church in America synod publications in the LCA sponsored contest last October (1981)." [63] In 1983, the total number of pages printed each year increased from 116 to 120, with some color pages in every issue.

Editor Shull in his annual reports to the synod regularly expressed his appreciation to the district reporters who channel news from congregations to the "Sandlapper Soul Scenes" columns and to the bishop and staff of synod for their support. In 1985, he wrote: "I am very grateful for the growing numbers of persons who are occasionally and regularly writing feature articles. . . . You enable us to have a broader coverage across the synod and to feature more often persons, events, and institutions that are meaningful in the life of our constituency." [64]

During the 1980's, there has also been more coverage of items pertaining to the life and work of the national church. As developments led to establishing the new Evangelical Lutheran Church in America in January 1988, the synodical paper devoted generous space to articles that informed the members of the synod of all phases of the merger and transition.

In 1987, the Rev. G. B. Corley marked 30 years as Business-Circulation Manager, and Editor Shull's 20th Anniversary passed in 1986. These tenures are indicative of the confidence placed in these men who are recommended by the Publications Committee of the Executive Board and elected by the synod in convention for two year terms. The Publications Committee is given the responsibility for the *South Carolina Lutheran*. It serves in an advisory/supervisory capacity. Decisions on purpose, policy, general guidelines, etc. are determined cooperatively by the publication's staff and the committee.

Pastor Shull also serves as the official synod correspondent for the LCA's publication, *The Lutheran*.

Other Programs

A Synod-Wide Bicentennial Banquet was held as part of the 1976 Convention at the Omar Shrine Temple in Charleston. Over 600 people attended this evening that included entertainment by the Madrigalians and the Jazz Ensemble from Newberry College, an address by the Rev. Dr. Robert J. Marshall, President of the LCA, and the fellowship of those assembled.[65]

The Executive Board authorized the commissioning of artist Leon Loard of Montgomery, Alabama, to paint a portrait of Dr. Herman W. Cauble.[66] The portrait was presented to the synod at a banquet as part of the 1979 Convention by the Rev. Earl H. Loadholdt on behalf of the Executive Board. Mrs. Cauble unveiled the portrait, and Dr. Cauble responded with words of appreciation.[67] The portrait was later hung in the Synod House.

The call process is one that affects every pastor and congregation. A resolution adopted by the 1981 Convention called on the Executive Board to appoint a special committee "to study the call procedures currently being used in our synod and other synods." [68] The Executive Board appointed James N. Hallman, chairman; the Rev. Henry M. Moody, Jr.; and Reid S. Wingard to this committee. They made a progress report to the 1982 Convention.[69] The Executive Board approved the final product, "Guides for the Call Process," set July 1, 1983 as the implementation date, and authorized the distribution of the guides to all pastors and church councils of the synod.[70] This guide has been a valuable tool to pastors, congregations, and the synod staff in working through the call process.

On March 28, 1984, a devastating tornado hit South Carolina with the most severe effect being felt in Newberry and Marlboro counties. Over $40,000 was channeled through the synod from congregations and individuals in the synod for disaster relief in the hard hit areas.[71]

A special ministry at the South Carolina Central Correctional Institution (CCI) in Columbia is carried out by a pastor of the South Carolina Synod and is supported by individuals and congregations of the synod. Having gradu-

Frankie San visits an inmate at CCI.

ated from LTSS in 1966 and having completed additional studies at the University of South Carolina, Kyuzo Miyaishi (Frankie San) was ordained by the synod in 1973 with a Call to Special Service as a "Tent Making Ministry" at CCI. Frankie San was born in Tokyo, Japan. At age 30, he became a Christian, graduated from Hosei University in Tokyo in 1961, and came to the United States to begin his studies at Columbia Bible College. In 1962, he transferred to LTSS and completed his internship at the Lutheran Children's Home of the South in Virginia.

Frankie San began visiting CCI while a student, proclaiming the message, "Christ loves you; I love you." Upon graduation, he began spending his days at the prison as an adult education instructor and later as a library assistant, teaching the prison illiterates the three R's, and introducing the meaning and value of brotherly love to the prison population. At Christmas, he dons a Santa Claus suit and distributes gifts he has collected from individuals and congregations. He regularly visits throughout the synod sharing the impact of his ministry, and publishes a regular Christmas report for the synod.

He has spent hours on Death Row, in the prison infirmary, in the Maximum Security section, and throughout the prison, writing letters to family and friends, giving encouragement, and proclaiming to all "Christ loves you; I love you." His legacy will continue through a foundation, currently valued at $800,000, established to ensure the continuation of this type of ministry.

The Merger

While continuing its full programs for ministry, the South Carolina Synod actively participated in the discussions and studies that would eventually lead to the formation of the Evangelical Lutheran Church in America in 1988, and to a restructuring of the South Carolina Synod organization. At the 1981 Convention of Synod, the Rev. Dr. Albert Haversat, Assistant to the Bishop of the LCA, addressed the convention on the proposals for Lutheran merger. At the conclusion of his report, an opinion poll was conducted, with 222 delegates voting in favor of a merger of the three Lutheran churches in some form, 44 preferring separate structures, and 11 undecided.[72] Reports from the Commission on Lutheran Unity (CNLC) to the 1982 and 1983 Conventions kept the synod informed of the progress that was being made, and of the direction that the merger was taking. At the 1984 Synod Convention, a more intensive review in small group forums and discussion on the floor of the convention were held concerning the CNLC report.[73] As a result of this, several sense motions expressing the feeling of the South Carolina Synod in convention were adopted for review by the CNLC. These motions included:

1) "that every ordained minister be a delegate in local and small regional assemblies, and ordained ministers have a fifty percent representation in the national and large regional assemblies" (243 for, 51 against, and 10 abstaining);

2) "that the quota aspect (which called for equal male and female representation) of the assemblies should be eliminated" (259 for, 44 against, and 8 abstaining);

3) "that the South Carolina Synod of the LCA supports only one level of specific ministry, that of those who are set apart for the ordained ministry, in the new Lutheran church;" at the same time affirming the priesthood of all believers and supporting those who serve in the lay ministry of the church (273 for, 19 against, and 4 abstaining);

4) "that membership in this church shall be defined as baptized members of its congregations" (280 for, 10 against, and 4 abstaining);

5) "that the new Lutheran Church should include an organization for women" (293 for, 0 against, and 5 abstaining);

6) "that a Lutheran Men's auxiliary be developed as a part of the new Lutheran Church" (297 for, 0 against, and 2 abstaining);

7) "that the congregation remain the sole base from which the new Lutheran church organizational structure is built" (135 for, 128 against, and 14 abstaining);

8) "that the CNLC establish an organization for youth as an auxiliary of the new Lutheran church" (298 for, 0 against, and 2 abstaining); and

9) "that, while we are against the quota system..., we support the spirit of the commission in attempting to establish fair representation of all persons," and ask the commission to carefully consider other alternatives that might achieve the same goals (202 for, 44 against, and 35 abstaining).

The voting was concluded with the adoption of a motion stating that the synod "confidently believes that God is guiding us to do His will in forming a new Lutheran church; we thank the commission for its laborious and diligent ministry; and we pray God's continuing guidance and blessing on their work." [74]

The Rev. Dr. H. George Anderson, a member of the CNLC, reported to the 1985 Convention on the work of the commission noting how they had responded to the input made through sense motions by the South Carolina and other synods. He also "reviewed the major areas where a consensus has not yet been reached." [75] Again, several sense motions were adopted by the convention:

1) "that satisfaction and pleasure be expressed concerning the proposed boundaries for Synod B of the Regional Center for Mission IX" (245 yes, 1 no);

2) "that it is the strong desire of the South Carolina Synod to have the state of Virginia included in Regional Center for Mission IX" (245 yes, 0 no);

3) "that it is the wish of the South Carolina Synod to share and be strengthened through our new Lutheran church with a relationship with the churches of the Carib-

bean, and that they be included within Regional Center for Mission IX" (243 yes, 2 no);

4) "that the ordering of ministry within the new Lutheran church reflect the primacy of the ministry of the whole people of God and the unique importance of the ordained ministry of Word and Sacrament. In synod assemblies, ordained ministers of Word and Sacrament be given voice and vote by virtue of their office and all commissioned ministers be considered lay persons eligible for election as delegates from their congregations. In the national assembly, commissioned ministers be considered as lay persons, eligible for election as lay delegates, and the delegates elected from the 'roster of ministers' be ordained ministers of Word and Sacrament. The new Lutheran church commit itself to the professional support of its commissioned ministers, allocating adequate resources for their preparation, continuing education, recognition, and constant support" (245 yes, 0 no); and

5) "that it is the sense of the South Carolina Synod to favor strongly Option A, which states 'each seminary be a seminary of this church, shall be incorporated, and shall be financed by synods of this church. Each seminary shall be governed by a Board of Regents, elected by the supporting synods, except that two regents shall be elected by the Division for Ministry from outside the supporting synods.'" (240 yes, 5 no).[76]

Earlier a motion had been adopted calling for all ordained ministers to have a vote at the Synod Assembly.[77]

By 1986, the intensity of the work toward merger had reached the point that the Executive Board appointed a task force to work for the transition of the South Carolina Synod into the new church.[78] This Transition Team, composed of the Rev. John L. Setzler, chairperson, with Mr. James N. Hallman, the Rev. David A. Donges, the Rev. Dr. James S. Aull, the Rev. Robert L. Dasher, and the Rev. Walter Wist as members, began a long and exhaustive process of looking at the synod in the framework of what the mission is, how the synod should be organized, and how it should operate. To do this, several task forces were appointed to work through the various aspects of the synod's ministry and organizational structure. At the 1986 Convention, three major steps were taken:

1) following the report of the CNLC, presented by the Rev. Dr. Reuben Swanson, Secretary of the LCA, the convention adopted a resolution strongly reaffirming the synod's support of the efforts being made to join together The Lutheran Church in America, The American Lutheran Church, and the Association of Evangelical Lutheran Churches, by January 1, 1988. The standing vote showed only 6 negative votes and 3 abstentions;[79]

2) the convention adopted a Mission Statement for the new South Carolina Synod of the Evangelical Lutheran Church as proposed by the Transition Team and amended;[80] and

3) a resolution approving the merger of the South Carolina Synod, LCA into the South Carolina Synod, ELCA was approved by more than the two-thirds vote required.[81]

Again several sense motions concerning the proposed merger were adopted by the convention. Five of them had been submitted by the Executive Board:

1) six recommendations concerning the governing documents of the ELCA, in view of the synod's understanding of the nature of the church, composed the first motion that was adopted (the actual motion adopted was a substitute motion offered from the floor);

2) a motion relating to the ordained ministry was adopted;

3) a motion calling for more articulate statements affirming a commitment to the development of ecumenical relationships was adopted;

4) support for inclusive representation in assemblies, councils, boards, committees, and governing bodies of the ELCA was approved; and

5) items related to the Pensions and Other Benefits were addressed.

Other sense motions included:

1) a recommendation "to include all ordained ministers as delegates at synod assemblies;"

2) a recommendation that the "constitution for congregations of the ELCA provide for the option of either the

pastor or a lay person serving as president of the congregation;"

3) a call for the reconsideration of the CNLC's "decision to locate the headquarters of the new church in Milwaukee;" and

4) a recommendation that the "primary location of the Lutheran Theological Southern Seminary continue to be in Columbia, South Carolina." [82]

All of this synod action, combined with the work of the CNLC, the South Carolina Synod Transition Team, and action by the conventions of the LCA, ALC, and AELC, and the Constituting Convention of the ELCA, culminated in the Constituting Convention of the South Carolina Synod of the ELCA at Newberry College on May 29-30, 1987. At this convention, the constitution, bylaws, and continuing resolutions were adopted; the Rev. Dr. James S. Aull was elected Bishop; Mrs. Mary Ann Shealy was elected Vice-President; the Rev. James W. Addy was elected Secretary; Mr. Raymond S. Caughman was elected Treasurer; members of the Synod Council and Boards of Trustees for Institutions and Committees of Consultation and Discipline were elected; representatives to the Regional Council were elected; a budget was adopted; the location of the synodical offices was approved; and other business was conducted by the voting delegates of lay men, lay women, certified lay professionals and clergy representing the 161 congregations of the LCA and the one congregation and one mission under the development of the ALC.[83]

Chapter Two—Committees

Committees carried out a large portion of the synod's work. As they engaged in the planning and execution of ministry programs for the synod, they enhanced the ability of congregations to function in its communities. Five of these committees were operational committees, and the membership included one lay person and one clergy person from each of the eight districts, and up to one additional person appointed by the bishop.[1]

American Missions

Bishop Cauble and the Rev. Joseph Holt break ground for the first unit at Cross and Crown, Florence.

The American Missions Committee, for which the bishop served as chairman, worked to foster and cultivate a "mission" spirit among the members of the South Carolina Synod. Working closely with the Division for Mission in North America's Regional Staff Person for South Carolina, this committee monitored and supported the development of mission congregations throughout South Carolina. It also provided financial aid for older congregations which were unable to maintain an adequate ministry on their own. Beyond that, this committee was also responsible for the summer ministry at camp sites in Myrtle Beach, and for supporting the Rural Mission, Incorporated, an ecumenical effort on John's Island.[2] The Rev. David F. Johnson served as the LCA's Deployed Staff

person for many years until his death in 1981. The Rev.
Boyce C. Whitener was later appointed to that position.

Evangelism

A major continuing project of the Evangelism Committee
has been the Carolinas' Evangelism Conference, sponsored
every two years by the North and South Carolina Synods.
These conferences began in 1966, and have brought to the
area some of the leading persons in the field of evangelism
to conduct workshops and worship services for congregational evangelism leaders. A Rally to open the conference
has been the highlight of this event for the past several
years. In 1973, a special evangelism emphasis called "Key
'73" was led by this committee. During this year, special
emphasis was placed on evangelism with workshops and
skillshops being held to equip members of the congregations with the skills needed to do person-to-person evangelism.[3] EvangALIVE in '75 was the key emphasis of evangelism that included five cluster clinics on inactive members,
prospective members, climate building, year round planning, and person to person witnessing.[4] A "Year Full of
Evangelism" was designated for 1984-85 to encourage every
congregation to develop an intentional program of evangelism to the unchurched, to the inactive, and for the integra-
tion of new members.[5] This followed action in 1976 when
the LCA and the ALC began working together on a joint
evangelism emphasis called Evangelical Outreach. An EO
coordinator was appointed by the synod with work to include emphasis on Bible study and witness through the
Word and Witness Program, the use of mass media for
evangelism, the training of parish callers, and the use of the
catechism for the training of new members.[6] EO was continued as a special project of the Evangelism Committee.
Additionally, this committee has regularly sponsored retreats, conferences, and workshops on evangelism, as well
as the publication of several evangelism guides for the congregational committees.[7]

Social Ministry

The Social Ministry Committee provided leadership for the synod and the congregations in various social areas and concerns that faced the people of South Carolina during these years. They did so by studying the issues and presenting resolutions to the synod conventions for adoption and implementation, and by developing programs for the congregations to use in their communities. Much of the work of this committee was done through the development of "task forces" and included work in areas of Native American Indian concerns, Ministry with the Aging, Alcohol and Drug Abuse, Literacy, Hospital Visitations, and many others. Three programs that the committee worked most diligently with deserve special note.

The committee sponsored the attendance of two deaf members of the synod at a Convention of the International Lutheran Deaf Association as a "first step" toward providing a broader ministry for the hearing impaired of South Carolina.[8] Work in this area grew until, with the assistance of DMNA, a mission congregation was organized in Columbia for people with impaired hearing and their families (see pages 2 and 169).

The Task Force on Minority Ministries began as a part of the Social Ministry Committee in 1979, and in 1985, became a committee of the synod (see page 9).

The most involved on-going ministry of the Social Ministry Committee has been that of child care. The 1970 Synod Convention directed the Executive Board to set up a special committee to study the synod's relationship with the Children's Home of the South and the availability of alternative services in South Carolina for child care. This committee recommended, and the conventions of synod in 1971 and 1972 approved, the withdrawal of support from the Children's Home because of the distance to the home in Virginia and because of comparable services available in South Carolina.[9] The synod's withdrawal became effective July 1, 1972, and the committee began to formulate its own program for child care in South Carolina. On January 1, 1974, the Social Ministry Committee began purchasing the services of the

Executive Director of the Lutheran Social Ministry Agency of Greater Columbia for one day per week as the Child Care Ministry Coordinator for the synod.[10] This relationship continued until the reorganization of the Social Ministry Agency into the Lutheran Social Services of Central South Carolina, which, while interested in the child care program, did not have the staff to carry out its work. The synod then hired a part-time person to carry out this ministry program.[11]

In addition to child care, the Social Ministry Committee became an advocate for many issues facing the South Carolina Legislature. One such issue revolved around concern over the fact that children could be legally bought and sold in South Carolina. A resolution expressing this concern was adopted by the 1984 Synod Convention (see page 10), and the result of this and other outcries from citizens of the state was the passage of measures to halt this practice and a review of the adoption laws of the state. The 1985 Convention approved a resolution in support of these actions.[12]

Also through the efforts of this committee, several special projects in the state have received grants for their work. Two examples of these are a grant of $10,000 to the South Carolina Literacy Association and a $3,000 grant to the Columbia Urban Service Center from the Board of Social Ministry, LCA.[13]

The on-going ministry team on aging expanded its ministry in the late 1980's. June 1983-May 1984 was adopted as "The Year of the Older Lutheran" by the 1983 Convention. As an affirmation of this recommendation, the convention rose and read a "Credo on Aging." [14] At the 1985 Convention, the Social Ministry Committee's recommendation calling for each congregation to appoint a "Senior Staffer" and to carefully review its program ministry with the aging was adopted.[15] Mr. Raymond L. Boozer served as Synod Senior Staffer,[16] and through his leadership, surveys of activities in the congregations for "seniors" were conducted; synod wide programs for "seniors," and workshops for developing programs for the aging in the congregation and community were held.

Educational Ministry

One of the most active of the synod's operational committees was that of Educational Ministry (formerly Parish Education). The oversight of many synodical programs that
affect every congregation, from teacher training to super-
vising the synod's media center, to supporting the camping
program at Lutheridge, became the primary concern of a
full-time staff person for many years. The Rev. Lloyd W.
Mitcham came to the South Carolina Synod as Executive
Director of Christian Education in 1968.[17] He served in this
area with expanded responsibilities to include Youth Ministry until his resignation in 1984.[18]

*A Vacation Church School work-
shop at Camp Kinard.*

Through the years this
committee has conducted
workshops, mini-labs, re-
treats, and other special
events to train Sunday
School teachers, to help Vacation Church School leaders, to promote confirmation
ministry programs, to help
develop educational ministry programs for all con-
gregations, and to cooperate
with the Division for Parish
Services in introducing new
curricular and programs to
congregations. Some of these activities and programs include seminars on confirmation ministry and First Communion instruction with the development by the LCA of a new
statement and policy regarding communion as early as the
fifth grade and with the introduction of new teaching materials for these classes.[19] A conference on Christian Family
Life was the highlight of 1979, featuring Dr. Charlie Shedd,
a well-known authority in that area.[20] Resource teams were
also developed to assist congregations and clusters of congregations in developing leadership training programs.[21] A
special observance of the 200th anniversary of the Sunday
School in 1980 included the Rev. Dr. James R. Crumley,

Bishop of the LCA, as the speaker for a rally day program.[22] "Strive for Five/Shoot for Ten" was a program that over 80 congregations participated in to stimulate the growth of the Sunday Church School program.[23] In 1984, acting on the recommendation of this committee, the synod convention passed a resolution calling for every congregation to appoint an Educational Ministry coordinator to oversee the entire educational ministry program within that congregation.[24]

The Church School Teacher of the Year Award was started in 1980 and named for Edwin Ricks in 1984. This award, given in memory of a South Carolinian who worked with the LCA in Parish Education for many years, is given annually to that person nominated by his or her congregation and selected by a panel, as the outstanding church school teacher for that year.[25]

The film library continued to be operated out of the Synod House "vault," [26] under the direction of this committee by the work of a part-time staff person, Mrs. Virginia Aull. Efforts have been made to keep the library up-to-date with religious film material, VCR equipment, and other materials and equipment for congregational use.

Dr. G. F. Schott conducts a worship service for the Scout Retreat in the newly constructed shelter.

Scouting has been an active part of the total ministry program for many of the congregations in the synod. For years, the Committee on Scouting has worked to promote scouting as a part of the Christian ministry for young boys and girls. This committee began a Boy Scout Retreat for Lutheran Scouts in South Carolina in 1970, and have held such a retreat at Camp Kinard in December of each year until 1987. At these weekend retreats, boys learn camping skills, share in recreation and fellowship, and have a Sunday Worship Service, with the offering each year going to the World Hunger Appeal. In 1971, the retreat had a bicentennial theme, with each troop presenting a skit on the theme. On May 16, 1987, a "work day" was held with troops camping out over the weekend of May 15-17. At this work day, a shelter was built to serve as the Retreat Center for the scouts. The 1987 Scout Retreat was scheduled for January 1988. The scouts had previously been responsible for getting the drive started to build the large shelter at Camp Kinard. Other "work days" have been held to clean up and repair the outpost area of Camp Kinard.

The Scout Committee is also responsible for promoting and publicizing the "Pro-Deo et Patria" and "God and Family" scout awards, and national scouting events. They have also been a consultant to congregations, encouraging them to make scouting a part of their ministry program. While many people have served diligently on this committee, the Rev. Dr. Fred Schott has been the leading advocate for scouting in the Lutheran Church in South Carolina.

Stewardship

The stewardship program of the synod has always been strong. Even in the difficult economic times of the state and

A stewardship display at synod convention.

the nation, the programs of the church have been carried out because of the generous support of the members of the synod, and because of the hard work of the Stewardship Committee. Since the Lutheran Church in America was formed in 1962, the South Carolina Synod has set as its top priority in the area of stewardship the full payment of the synod's benevolence quota to the LCA. That quota has been paid by 100% and more every year. The synod's Stewardship Committee regularly communicated with the congregations and members of synod through a newsletter called "Ship Shape," and conducted workshops for congregational members and pastors. Mr. Thomas J. O'Brien became the LCA's deployed staff person for stewardship in the Southeast in 1975 and made his office at the synod house, serving other synods in the area as well.

In addition to the operational committees, several standing committees worked within the synod to provide program support and leadership for the congregations and pastors. These committees were appointed by the bishop with the approval of the Executive Board.[27]

Worship

The Committee on Worship provided pastors and congregations with much valuable information throughout the years, as well as leadership for various special worship opportunities in the synod and the districts. District workshops gave worship leaders and participants from various congregations the opportunity to come together and hear about ways of enhancing congregational worship, developing choirs, and providing ways in which the laity can become more involved in worship leadership. They also gave members an opportunity to share ideas about what was happening in worship in the various congregations, providing new ideas for others. Each year the Worship Committee was called upon to plan and coordinate the Ordination Service for the synod as well as the Service of Holy Communion at each synod convention. Some years these two services

Members of the Worship Committee line up participants for the proces-sional of the Opening Worship Service of a synod convention.

were combined at the synod convention; at other times they were held separately. The committee also provided displays and forums at synod conventions on worship; published articles in the *South Carolina Lutheran* on worship; helped sponsor conferences on Worship, Music and the Arts; provided each congregation with a listing of hymns that were appropriate for each Sunday of the three year cycle, as well as those Sundays of the Lesser Festivals;[28] and began a Worship Notebook for each congregation about the seasonal worship opportunities.

The biggest project of this committee was the introduction of the *Lutheran Book of Worship* to the congregations of the synod in 1978. The arrival of this "green book" weighing 2 lbs. and 6 ozs.[29] was greeted with mixed emotions throughout the synod. While the *Service Book and Hymnal* had been in use for only twenty years, many people had developed a deep attachment to its forms of worship and hymn selections and were reluctant to make the change to the "green book." However, with the well organized and trained work of several leadership groups, the transition into this new book of worship was very smooth and complete. The use of the three settings within the book is widely divided throughout the synod, with some congregations using more than one setting during the year.

In 1982, the synod adopted a resolution encouraging all congregations to provide ways for each active member to "invite, encourage, and bring others who are inactive or unchurched to worship." [30]

World Missions

The Rev. James L. Brady, his wife, Lynne, and their children, Mary and Anna, at the Service of Commissioning held on May 25, 1986. Pastor Brady serves as a pastor-teacher, and Mrs. Brady serves in a ministry program with the deaf. Other participants in the service were (pictured in the background) Pastors Larry Bost, Henri Bishop, and Robert Dasher.

While world missions continued to be a strong part of the Lutheran church's ministry and was widely supported by congregations within the South Carolina Synod, the emphasis of this ministry shifted from Americans serving in these mission fields to local nationals providing the leadership for the Lutheran church in their own countries. As a result, the number of missionary families from the United States has decreased, and since 1971, only seven missionary families from South Carolina have served overseas. In 1986, the synod celebrated the commissioning of the Rev. and Mrs. James L. Brady as missionaries.[31] Missionary families from the synod have included:

The Rev. and Mrs. Henri Bishop in Malaysia and Singapore serving as a pastor, returning home in 1979;

Mr. and Mrs. Stanley Frick serving as teachers in Japan until 1973:

Mr. and Mrs. Herbert W. Heyse serving as teachers in Tanzania until 1978;

The Rev. and Mrs. Jerry C. Livingston still serving as a pastor in Japan;

The Rev. and Mrs. William Peery serving as a seminary professor in India;

Mr. and Mrs. Larry Freeze serving as a maintenance manager in Liberia until their return home in 1986;

The Rev. and Mrs. James Brady currently serving as a pastor in Malaysia.

Although the overseas missionary scene has changed, support for the world missions program has remained high through the work of the World Missions Committee of synod and the individual congregations that support these missionaries. In 1983, for example, the South Carolina Synod had the highest percentage of congregations in the LCA supporting overseas missionaries through Designated Advanced Gifts.[32] This support continues as congregations provide funds and personal contact in support of the missionaries and their ministry. Congregation support for world missions through Designated Advanced Gifts in 1986 was $93,300.[33]

In 1977, a Global Missions Event was held at Newberry College. Sponsored by six synods in the Southeast in cooperation with DMNA and DWME of the LCA, this event focused on the work of missionaries and the support needed from the American congregations. Almost 500 people attended this conference.[34] In 1984, the synod adopted a resolution challenging each congregation to receive a special Reformation Offering amounting to at least $1.00 per confirmed member that would be divided equally between the development of new congregations in the United States and support of the world missions work of the LCA.[35]

A bequest from the estate of James M. Holman was received by the synod in 1979. Parcels of land in Calhoun County were sold, and the proceeds ($151,660.03) were invested with the interest of this fund designated for the support of missionary work in Japan.[36] The synod has had other close ties with the work of missionaries in Japan. In 1971, Dr. and Mrs. Chitose Kishi visited South Carolina. Dr. Kishi, a 1926 graduate of Southern Seminary, is former President of the Japan Evangelical Lutheran Church and Japan Lutheran Theological College and Seminary. His visit was sponsored by the Board of World Missions and their Missionary-in-Residence program. Dr. Kishi taught at Southern Seminary in the spring quarter of 1971 and visited throughout the synod with the World Missions Committee making those arrangements.[37]

A delegation of visitors from the Lutheran Church in Japan made a "roots" tour of the southern United States in the fall of 1983. The visit was developed because the Japanese Lutheran Church had its beginnings through missionaries sent by the United Synod of the South, commissioned at services held at St. John, Charleston. Again the World Missions Committee served as hosts for part of this tour.[38]

In 1986, a group of 18 girls and 2 teachers from the high school in Kumamoto, Japan visited in the synod for two weeks, staying with host families in the Charleston and Columbia areas.[39]

World Hunger

A discussion of the World Hunger program.

Brought to the forefront by news reports from especially hard hit countries, a task force was set up in 1974 to direct the work of the synod in the area of world hunger. Congregations and individuals were strongly encouraged to participate in the fight against hunger throughout the world. In 1974, approximately $27,000 was given[40] with that amount rising to over $66,000 in 1975.[41] In 1982, the task force became a committee of synod,[42] and with the World Hunger Program extended through 1990—a decade of commitment—support for the program from the South Carolina Synod reached a high of $241,000 in 1985.[43] For several years the synod led the LCA in per capita giving to World Hunger.

In 1984, the committee published a World Hunger Resource Book for all congregations,[44] and in 1985, co-sponsored with Southern Seminary a conference on root causes of hunger to educate people to the condition and its causes.[45] While hunger remains a severe problem throughout the world, including parts of the United States and South Carolina, this committee has continued to educate members of the synod's congregations about the needs and means of meeting those needs through the World Hunger Program.

Professional Leadership

Preparing professional leaders for the church continued to be a vital part of the synod's overall ministry. This work was done by three different committees whose names and structures changed during this period primarily because of restructuring at the national level, but that in some form helped prepare persons for the full-time ministry, helped full-time church workers continue their education and sharpen their skills, and provided guidelines and support for financial compensation packages for pastors.

The Professional Leadership Preparation Committee was a combination of the Church Vocations and Examining Committees.[46] This committee worked with people, sometimes as early as high school, who felt the desire to pursue some type of church vocation as their life's work. Contact with these individuals continued through their college and seminary years by conducting interviews, providing appropriate testing, and making endorsements for entrance into seminary. Their work also included the final examination of students before certifying to the synod that they met all requirements for ordination.

Providing Continuing Education for clergy and lay professionals was the primary task of the Professional Leadership Services Committee, formerly the Continuing Education Committee.[47] In 1972, Pastors' Retreats at Camp Kinard were well received,[48] and the committee began mak-

Bishop Cauble talks with Pastors Paul Slice (right) and Buzz Van Horne (left), during a break at a pastors' retreat.

ing them an annual event, expanding them to include lay professionals. The committee also encouraged congregations to provide time and funds for these continuing education events, and encouraged each pastor to receive three Continuing Education Units each year.[49] The retreats offered opportunities for study, spiritual reflection, skill development, and fellowship. They attracted many pastors and a number of outstanding leaders. The committee also sponsored pastor/spouse conferences, pre-retirement seminars, first-year-in-ministry retreats, church management seminars, orientation workshops for new pastors in the synod, and professional counseling, free and on a confidential basis, for pastors and spouses.

For several years the Pastoral Support Committee annually compiled data on the compensation of pastors and reported their findings to the synod convention and congregations, making recommendations about budget considerations for pastoral support. Of particular concern were the number of pastors at the lower end of the compensation scale. The 1971 Synod Convention directed the Pastoral Support Committee to address itself to the question of the adequacy of pastors' compensation, and to study and make recommendations for the same. In 1970, the average total compensation was $8,759.[50] Following this mandate, the committee developed a Guideline for Minimum Pastoral Compensation. At the 1977 Convention, several pastors submitted a three part resolution through the Committee on Reference and Counsel. Part I recommended the establishment of a parish-pastor relations committee in each congregation with responsibilities outlined, and Part III recommended that $25,000 be added to the 1978 Budget to be used to supplement pastors' salaries which fell below the recommended levels, and that the Pastoral Support Committee develop guidelines for supplementing pastors' salaries. These two parts were adopted. Part II, which was referred to the Pastoral Support Committee, set forth a compensation scale that included a base salary (based on years of ordained ministry and size of congregation), housing and utilities, business and professional expenses, and benefits.[51] The 1977 Convention also adopted a resolution calling for the Executive Board to give top priority to an allocation at the end of the year for the establishment of an emergency fund for pastoral support. As a result, the Executive Board authorized the President of synod to inform pastors of such funds and requesting that pastors present their needs. In January 1978, $15,000 was set aside for this emergency fund. The Pastoral Support Committee sent a letter to the 35 lowest paid pastors informing them that supplementary funds were available for those who needed it. Six responses were received. Two indicated that they did not need such supplemental support, but that the discussion of pastoral compensation with their councils had proven to be beneficial. Financial supplements were given to four pastors plus two mission pastors recommended by the American Missions Committee.[52] The Pastoral Support Committee developed guidelines for a "Pastoral Service Committee in the Congregation," a "Minimum Pay Package" for 1979 with challenge goals, and "Guidelines to Supplement Pastors' Salaries." These were presented to the 1978 Convention and were adopted.[53] Since that convention, the committee has annually submitted "Recommended Pay Packages" with challenge goals. The committee has also been active in providing clergy and congregations with information concerning the impact of Social Security and tax law changes on the pastoral support package.

Parish Life and Ministry Development

Parish Life and Ministry Development (P.L.M.D.) began with a retreat in 1973, and was so well received that the Executive Board was encouraged to establish a committee to provide assistance to congregations through the P.L.M.D. program.[54] This program is a "combined effort of congregations, synods, and churchwide agencies to develop parish

A PLMD committee at work.

life and ministry in a comprehensive way. The heart of the experience is an on-going process of planning and implementing, out of which parish life and ministry emerges and is continually renewed." In 1976, a special committee appointed to study the need for additional synod staff recommended that the synod employ a part-time staff person in the area of P.L.M.D.[55] Dr. D. J. Haigler was employed as the P.L.M.D. staff person in 1977[56] and served until 1984 when he was succeeded by Mrs. Jackie Lybrand.[57] Church council cluster retreats and individual council retreats in the local setting, as well as the use of LCA resources such as *Renewing*, have been focal points for the P.L.M.D. work.

Camp and Conference Ministries

Camp and conference ministries within the territory of the South Carolina Synod had for two decades been largely limited to the ministry of Lutheridge. However, in 1967, 100 acres were purchased and 100 acres received as a gift from the O. R. Boozer estate.[58] On this 200 acre site near Leesville, S. C. has been developed the Karl W. Kinard Conference Center named to honor the long-time president of the synod. The desire of the synod was to provide year-round facilities at which groups within the synod and congregations could conduct retreats, conferences, meetings, and learning experiences. Development plans for Kinard Conference Center were presented to the 1969 Synod Convention. The convention authorized the promotion of these plans and the borrowing of $150,000 to construct the main conference center building.[59] The conference building and first cottage were built in 1970 with the cottage being a gift of the Lutheran Men of the synod. The men also contributed labor and resources to enlarge an existing lake and construct a second lake.[60]

Eagerness to have such a conference center was shown by the more than 3,500 people in 94 groups who used Kinard Conference Center in its first year of operation. The Rev. L. W. Mitcham, Jr., synodical Secretary of Christian Education, handled reservations for using the center. In January 1971, Mr. and Mrs. Simmie Amick began duties as resident caretaker and cooks. The second cottage constructed was provided by four Columbia churches: St. Paul, Reformation, St. Andrew, and Ebenezer. Two more cottages were donated from the estate of Mrs. Clarence H. Wertz of Orangeburg.[61] A dedication service for all the facilities at Kinard Conference Center constructed up to that time was held on April 16, 1972.[62]

The youth of the synod began an effort in 1972 to raise funds for the construction of a swimming pool. Their goal was to collect a dollar from every confirmed member within the synod. Over a thousand youth and adults gathered in August, 1973, for groundbreaking services for the pool.[63] The pool was used the next summer and dedicated on Sep-

The swimming pool at Camp Kinard is dedicated.

tember 8, 1974. Final cost of the pool was nearly $40,000.

A fifth cottage, completed in 1973, was a gift of five West Columbia area churches: St. David, Mt. Tabor, Emmanuel, Our Saviour, and Mt. Hermon. The sixth and last cottage was constructed in 1974-75 and was a gift from an anonymous donor in honor of Dr. Carl B. Caughman.[64]

The family camping center was first used in 1973. This area with 13 campsites and bathhouse was provided by churches in the Ridge area including Wittenberg, Leesville; Grace, Gilbert; St. Peter, Batesburg; Faith, Batesburg; Cedar Grove, Leesville; and St. Mark and Corinth, Prosperity.[65] A tennis and volleyball court was also developed at this time. The outpost area was cleared and developed by Boy Scout troops from across the synod. The large picnic shelter and nearby restroom in the outpost area were partially provided by a one-time appeal in the congregations in 1975.

A change in the administration of Kinard Conference Center occurred in August 1973, when Pastor Harold G. Skinner accepted the call to become pastor of Wittenberg, Leesville. Involved in the call was an agreement with the executive board of synod to purchase 20% of his time to serve as Coordinator of Kinard Conference Center.[66]

The 1975 Synod Convention approved a synod wide appeal for Camp and Conference Ministries to begin no earlier than 1978.[67] In order not to begin too closely after the start of the LCA's Strength for Mission appeal, the 1977 Convention set the time for the Camp and Conference Appeal to begin its congregational phase in the summer of 1979 with a 24-month pledge period.[68] Its basic goal was $750,000. The challenge goal was $1,000,000.

The Lodge Complex at Camp Kinard is dedicated by (left to right): Pastors Harold Skinner, Camp Coordinator; James S. Aull, Synod Secretary; James W. Addy, Chairman, Camp and Conference Ministries Committee.

Incarnation, Columbia, provided funds for the building of the first unit in the Lodge Complex at Kinard Conference Center. The unit, constructed in 1978, consisted of four motel-type rooms with 2 double beds each, individual room heating/cooling, and private baths.

Mr. and Mrs. Simmie Amick resigned their positions at Kinard Conference Center in May 1979. Mr. and Mrs. Harold Benson began nearly two years of service as Food Preparation Director and assistant. Mr. Edward O. Barber served as resident Caretaker from September 1979 through December 1981. The resignation of Pastor Skinner as Coordinator effective December 31, 1981, had led to a decision by the Management Committee to seek a resident Camp Director. The duties of administering the conference center had grown too large to be handled by only 20% of a person's time. Mr. Jerry A. Freeze was chosen as Camp Director, a position which combined administrative and maintenance duties. He assumed these duties on April 1, 1982.

Along with a $30,000 gift from the Self Foundation of Greenwood, funds from the camping appeal provided the second unit in the Lodge Complex at Kinard Conference Center. Appeal funds were also used to pave a major portion of the road system at Camp Kinard. During 1981, Kinard Conference Center received "through a very generous arrangement by Miss Laura Brodie" ownership of an additional 93.5 acres of land adjacent to the conference center.[69] Use of the conference center grew in 1981 to over 8,300 people in 249 different groups. The third unit in the Lodge Complex at Kinard Conference Center consists of four bedrooms and a meeting room, which can be converted into two bedrooms at a future date. This unit was constructed in 1982.[70] One of the bedrooms is being used as an office. In 1982, the residence on the grounds at Kinard was vastly remodeled in order to be suitable for the Camp Director's home. Construction of a maintenance building was also begun that year.

A one-week Lutheridge Satellite camp for junior campers was held for the first time in 1982. Other special summer programs at this time included a camping program known as Camp Kemo for children with cancer, two camps for mentally retarded children, and camps for autistic and diabetic children.[71]

Twenty-five acres across Two Notch Road from the entrance to Kinard Conference Center were purchased in 1985 to assure an attractive entrance to the center. A small picnic shelter adjacent to the main conference center and a recreational field near the outpost shelter were added at Kinard Conference Center in 1985. In 1986, Mr. Jerry Freeze resigned as Camp Director, and Mr. Herbert Loadholdt became the new Director in April 1987.[72]

Upon the urging of the Charleston area pastors, the Executive Board considered the purchase of the former property of St. Mark, Sullivan's Island for use as a retreat center. The congregation had relocated to the Isle of Palms. The executive board recommended to the 1974 Synod Convention that the former church property be purchased for $22,500 and two adjacent lots owned by the town be purchased for $600 each. The convention approved the recommendation.[73] Volunteers from Charleston area churches prepared the former parish building for use as a retreat center and maintained it as well. This temporary center, therefore, was self-supporting at the low rate of $1 per day per person or $5 per group for day use.

Plans for developing the Sullivan's Island property into a

retreat center were rejected by that town's zoning commission. Thus, other suitable property was sought in the Charleston area. The 1978 Synod Convention approved the purchase of 1.47 acres of land at the corner of 21st Avenue and Palm Boulevard on the Isle of Palms at a net cost of $100,000. The Town Council of the Isle of Palms had given permission to develop the property as a retreat center.[74] The executive board was authorized to sell the Sullivan's Island property.

General concepts and plans for the Coastal Retreat Center were approved by the 1980 Synod Convention. It also authorized the borrowing of $400,000 to complete the center.[75] Groundbreaking for the new Coastal Retreat Center

Ground is broken for the Coastal Retreat Center by (left to right): Mr. John S. Rodenberg and the Rev. E. Armand Shealy, members of the building committee; Mr. Charles A. Curl, representative of Stanley Smith and Sons, Inc., contractors; Bishop Cauble; the Rev. Eugene Kern, member of the building committee; Mr. Harry Stoudenmire, chairman of the building committee; and the Rev. James W. Addy, chairman of the Management Committee for Camp and Conference Ministries.

was held on March 1, 1981. The completed center contains twenty bedrooms with the necessary meeting rooms, kitchen, etc. It was first used in January 1982, and was dedicated on March 27, 1982. Groups using the Coastal Retreat Center provide their own linens and prepare their own meals. In its first year of operation, nearly 3,000 people in 117 groups used the center. Mr. and Mrs. Edwin (Kathryn) Mohrmann donated three years' service as managers of the retreat center.

Use of the Coastal Retreat Center grew to over 250 days in 1983. Such use allowed payments on the debt and the construction of a recreational court costing approximately $19,000. Mr. and Mrs. Robert (Marlene) Park served as managers of the retreat center for seven months in 1985. Mr. and Mrs. Cy (Martha) Kaemmerlen assumed the duties of the managers in November 1985.

The executive board, late in 1985, approved the installation of an elevator at the Coastal Retreat Center in order to better accommodate all of the various groups which use the center. In 1987, they also approved the purchase of the property at 2105 Palm Blvd., adjacent to the center, to be

The Coastal Retreat Center.

used as a residence for the managers of the center. Through the gift of Mr. and Mrs. Walter A. Sigman, Jr. of Clinton, this purchase was completed, and the residence was named "The Sigman House" in their honor.[76]

For several years, management of the camp and conference centers had been the responsibility of an appointed committee. At the 1977 Convention, a resolution was adopted calling for the Executive Board to give serious consideration "to the establishment of an elected board of trustees for the Karl W. Kinard Conference Center and/or the Sullivan's Island Retreat Center ... to oversee their administration." [77] In 1978, first reading approval was given to a constitutional amdendment establishing a nine member Management Committee for Camp and Conference Ministries elected by the convention.[78] Final approval was given at the 1979 Convention,[79] and the first committee was elected. This committee has since had the responsibility for overseeing the camp and conference ministries of the synod.

Certified Lay Professionals

An important support group within the church's ministry program has been the lay people who work in the church in various ministry areas. They have worked in areas such as music, educational ministry, youth ministry, visitation, administration, etc. The use of these lay professionals has grown through the years, so that some congregations have full-time persons, and some congregations have several part-time persons. By meeting guidelines established by the LCA, these persons could become "Certified Lay Professionals" (CLP's). In 1983, the Executive Board authorized the Professional Leadership Preparation Committee to study the relationship of the CLP's to the synod.[80] The 1985 Convention approved an amendment to the synod's constitution giving CLP's seat and voice at conventions.[81]

Campus Ministry

The campus ministry program of the synod works to provide Lutheran youth at the non-Lutheran colleges and universities in South Carolina with a program designed to strengthen the faith and maintain the worship experiences of these Lutheran students. While the programs are varied throughout the state because of the numbers of students involved and the setting in which they live and study, the overall program can be divided into three basic groups.

At the University of South Carolina in Columbia, the synod maintains a fulltime ministry through a Lutheran Campus Pastor. In 1968, Pastor Carl Ficken resigned from that position,[82] having seen the growth of Lutheran campus ministry at the university and at Columbia College grow both in quality and quantity. The synod, in cooperation with the National Lutheran Campus Ministry, an agency of the LCA and ALC, continued the strong pastoral leadership at these two schools by first using two seminarians, Hollis Miller and Larry Yoder,[83] and then by calling the Rev. Robert Dasher as the Lutheran Campus Pastor for the Columbia area, beginning his work in January 1969.[84]

In the seventies, USC experienced tremendous growth and transition. The Campus Center and ministry provided a way for many students to make the change from home to campus. The center became a "home away from home." Student unrest during the seventies made its way to USC, and campus ministry served a mediating role, and the Lutheran Center made headlines as students operated a first aid station during the disturbances of 1970.

The campus pastor during this time continued to meet with a small group of students at Columbia College. Professor D. J. Haigler, a faculty member at Columbia College, provided leadership for the campus ministry.[85]

As one examines the first part of the seventies, the ministry at USC served many students through meals provided by local congregations, challenging programs, a warm and beautiful center which was a home built in the early 1900's, innovative liturgies, opportunities for service projects, pastoral counseling, contact with international students and interracial exchanges, and relationship with national and international student movements.

A dramatic threat came to the ministry in 1974. USC needed the Campus Center property at 1529 Pendleton Street. For many, the Center was more than a building; there were students who felt that they would not have survived college if it had not been for the Center; and many students met their spouses at the Center. Unfortunately, the synod had no recourse due to the university's power of eminent domain. However, the issue of what the property was worth had to be settled in court. A jury of the Richland County Court of Common Pleas directed the university to pay the synod $117,500 for damages. After deducting attorney's fees and other costs related to selling the building, the balance was divided between the synod and the National Lutheran Campus Ministry based on the percentage each had contributed to the original purchase of the building. The synod has invested its share of $55,884.58 with the income being used to help finance the ministry's annual operations.[86]

A tradition called "Fireside" was last held on December 15, 1974, and helped a group of over one hundred say thanks for the past and goodbye to the building as, through tears, they looked to the future. Beverly Alexander, then a student and now a campus pastor in North Carolina, wrote both an obituary and a birth announcement as the Lutheran Ministry moved from its Center to the Wesley Foundation. Appearing in the *South Carolina Lutheran* were these words: "All it took was one man to attach a cable—another to drive a massive machine and the building which was once the Lutheran Student Center at the University of South Carolina soon became past history. What man had created, man also destroyed. The building has served with dignity and warmth." [87]

For the next few years Lutheran Campus Ministry was housed at the Wesley Foundation cooperating in some programs, in addition to offering distinctive programs. During this period, the Lutheran Campus Ministry sign was replaced with one that read "The ELM Center" with ELM being formed by the first letters of the three denominations housed in the Wesley Foundation—Episcopal, Lutheran, and Methodist.[88] The ELM ministry provided an excellent environment for students to deepen their own traditions but also to learn from each other. Worship was always a strong commitment for the ministry. Study groups, support groups, counseling, social activities, leadership development, service projects, faculty luncheons, seminars for clergy, retreats, forums, and Bible study all helped shape the ministry from the middle seventies to the eighties.[88]

At the end of 1984, Pastor Dasher resigned,[89] and, again, the ministry was served by seminarian Shawn Norris until the new Campus Pastor, John Hougen, began his work in August 1986.[90] Prior to Pastor Hougen's arrival, the ELM ministry was dissolved with the Episcopal Church moving their ministry to the recently completed Diocesan House in Columbia. Thus began "The Lutheran/United Methodist Campus Ministry" [91] which has continued to provide ministry to the university's students as they struggle with life's development in a university setting.

At Clemson University, the Campus Ministry program is a cooperative one with the University Lutheran Church in Clemson. With support from the synod's Campus Ministry Committee, this program has grown with the addition of a second staff person as they continue to minister to a growing Lutheran population at the University and in the community. Through the years, an active Lutheran Student Movement has provided the framework for many programs for the Lutheran students at Clemson. Special programs for "Young Marrieds," [92] special worship services for the students, weekly Bible study programs, and retreats, [93] plus shared programs with the congregation, have made the campus ministry program at Clemson an active and important ministry of the synod. (See University Church, page 264).

At other colleges within the state, part-time staff persons and contact pastors from local congregations have provided ministry to the Lutheran students "at home, away from home." Winthrop, The Citadel, and the College of Charleston have part-time staff persons, while contact pastors have provided ministry and program support at Claflin, South Carolina State, Furman, Converse, Wofford, Erskine, Lander, Coker, Limestone, Presbyterian, and Francis Marion. All of this work is done in cooperation with the Division of Campus Ministry of the Lutheran Council in the U.S.A., and its representative, Dr. Robert Walker. [94]

Communications

Publicity for major synod events was coordinated through the synod office by the Publicity Committee. This committee was especially responsible for the distribution of news releases to the major news centers of the state before, during, and after each convention. In 1975, the committee arranged for each delegate to have a picture taken with a representative of the synod for publication in the hometown newspaper. That year the committee also began the publication of "Convention Notes" which was mailed to each delegate and congregation immediately following the convention giving a synopsis of the convention's actions.[95] A brochure "Lutherans in Action" was published by the committee in 1976.[96] In 1986, the name of the committee was changed to the Committee on Communications, reflecting more accurately its duties and responsibilities.[97] That year, a workshop on the preparation of church newsletters and general news releases was conducted.[98]

Youth Ministry

Youth in recreation at a retreat at Camp Kinard.

Throughout these years, the Youth Ministry Committee has been responsible for coordinating programs within the synod "to provide opportunities for young people and adults to better equip themselves"[99] to live within their communities as a part of God's people. Until 1978, there was no youth organization in the synod, and this committee held the sole responsibility for providing these programs. The Migrant Ministry program, youth rallies and conferences, training conferences for adult leaders, coordinating regional youth gatherings, leading the project to raise funds for the swimming pool at Camp Kinard, were all a part of this committee's work to "expand and develop ministries with youth"[100] so that they could be more effective in their congregations and in their daily lives. The addition of the Youth Staffer enabled the committee to expand its ministry with and for youth.

In response to convention action, the committee appointed an Implementation Committee to establish a state-wide youth organization.[101] This was completed with the organization of the Lutheran Church Youth in August 1978 (see page 60).

Lutheran youth participate in MR Camp at Camp Kinard.

In 1987, as a part of the transition process relating to the synod's becoming a part of the ELCA, the youth ministry program was thoroughly studied, and recommendations for modifications of the program were adopted. The major change was the employment of a part-time Youth Ministry Coordinator for the synod, in place of the Youth Staffer program. Mrs. Nancy Padgett began her work in September 1987,[102] working through this committee and with the LCY to maintain consistency in the youth ministry program in the synod, and to facilitate youth programs through "networking"—putting people with needs in touch with people with the appropriate skills to meet those needs. The Youth Ministry Committee has continually provided programs for youth, enabling them to experience opportunities for learning, fellowship, and leadership development.

Ministry of the Laity

The 1984 LCA Convention adopted a ministry statement on "God's People Called to Ministry" as a result of their baptism, through their vocations, using the different gifts of the Holy Spirit in their daily lives. As a part of this statement, each synod was called upon to appoint a task force to assist the church in its support of God's people in their ministry in the world, with attention to ways in which the programs, priorities, and emphasis of the church can support that ministry. In South Carolina, such a task force was appointed, and they set several goals for their work.

They included: a process of identifying the laity; deepening the understanding of ministry in daily life and exploring ways to support that ministry; affirming the ministry of the laity in its various expressions; and sharing that ministry. The task force immediately began to plan, discuss, and implement these goals by sending publicity to pastors, LCW and LM presidents, and others concerning the Ministry of the Laity; making presentations at district meetings and synod conventions; promoting the third Sunday of November as Laity Sunday; conducting a workshop at Newberry College on February 16, 1985; and encouraging pastors and lay people to attend a leadership conference on "Connections," a word and witness type of study designed for use in the congregation for 32 weeks. A seminar on "God's People in Ministry" in September 1986, with Dr. Marilyn Ascarza from LTSS as the leader, provided participants with ideas on the ministry of the laity, discussion groups, devotions, and Bible Study.

There has been a great increase in interest and participation in lay ministry within the synod. More congregations have participated in Laity Sunday, received materials, heard presentations at district meetings, attended forums and seminars, used the Living Faith Series, *Monday's Ministries*, and other ministry of laity books, and in general raised their awareness of the laity and their role within the church's ministry programs.[103]

Blue Ribbon Committee

In 1972, the Blue Ribbon Committee was established to help coordinate the ministry programs of the synod. Composed of the district deans, the chairpersons of each committee of synod, the editor of the *South Carolina Lutheran*, and the presidents of the auxiliaries, the committee had an annual retreat with the officers and staff of the synod at Camp Kinard. Here program planning and discussion of the ministry profile of the synod led to coordination of programs and scheduling as well as planning for synodwide and district meetings. This committee provided a great deal of "feed in" to the executive board throughout the years.

Chapter Three—Auxiliaries

Among the most active people within the synod are those persons involved in the three auxiliaries—Lutheran Church Women, Lutheran Church Youth, and Lutheran Men. As a part of the individual congregations, they provide opportunities for small group programs and discussions, fellowship, worship, and program support for the various ministries within the congregation. They have been an effective way for members to find avenues of ministry in their church and community. As a part of the South Carolina Synod, these auxiliaries provide support for the ongoing ministry of the church with special emphasis in certain ministry areas. They are also a valuable resource for persons with leadership skills and experience. South Carolina has been especially fortunate to have three very active and effective auxiliaries within its ministry program.

Lutheran Church Women

Since 1962 when it was reorganized, the Lutheran Church Women has been growing, working, and serving with love, concern, and enthusiasm. Through the years new programs have been developed by the auxiliary. Increasing importance has been placed on service to the people of the world through involvement in social concerns. South Carolina Lutheran Women have been in leadership roles in the literacy program in the state since 1962. They have sponsored workshops for training tutors, have served as tutors themselves, have aided the program financially, and have cooperated with the State Literacy Association. Like the LCA, the women's organization has been deeply concerned about world hunger, peace, justice, and fair treatment for all human beings. Projects to send material help to specific groups in mission fields, within the state or through Lutheran World Federation, have been supported by the organization in recent years. Migrant missions, ministry to the deaf, and aid to Native Americans have been areas of

Bernice Shealy, Gloria Rast and Betty Bradley pack sewing kits made by the LCW.

particular interest in this state. Because of the wide scope of social missions, Key Women have been named for each district to assist the unit committee and to aid the local organizations in this area of work. Wide interest in social ministry expresses the continuing active love and concern which have marked women's work in South Carolina from its beginning.

Communication between the synodical organization and the local groups has been a challenge throughout the history of women's work in South Carolina. However, in recent years there has been a more concentrated effort by LCW to improve lines of communication. Since 1973, the synodical unit has published its own newsletter. Known as the *GOOD-NEWSletter*, it is published four times a year. In addition, LCW information has been included in each issue of the *South Carolina Lutheran*. In 1970, the unit board began each year to send the *Calendar of Events* which has served as a reminder to local groups of important events, dates, and other suggestions to help in planning activities at the local level. Various publications, sent regularly from the auxiliary to unit and local leaders, have provided a constant flow of information and guidance. *Lutheran Women*, the auxiliary's national magazine, has been widely read by women from 73% of the congregational organizations. District assemblies, held each fall, and the annual conventions have not only been wonderful sources of information but have provided inspiration and joy which cannot be measured.

The Lutheran women of the South Carolina Unit, like the synod itself, have established an outstanding record of stewardship. Although there have been a few rough years in financial giving (usually corresponding with periods of difficulty in the economy), there have been several years when the SCLCW gave more than 100% of budgeted funds to the auxiliary while meeting all obligations at home. Probably the real key to the stewardship of the women has been the overwhelming proportion of contributions given to "others" as contrasted with monies retained for the use of the congregational groups. At the convention of SCLCW, delegates adopted a 1987 budget of $88,975.00, with $75,625.00 to be spent for "others."[1]

Members of the LCW put their Thankoffering in the Treasure Chest during worship at their convention.

One phase of giving which has grown tremendously since its beginning has been "Thankoffering." When Lutheran Church Women was organized in 1962, the decision was made to combine all offerings into one gift. But in 1970, the idea of a special offering to be received during Lent and Thanksgiving was adopted by SCLCW. So successful was the idea that at the National Triennial Convention in 1971, the auxiliary adopted South Carolina's idea as a channel for "special gifts." Today the ingathering of Thankoffering has become one of the highlights of each convention. At the 1987 convention this offering amounted to over $20,800.[2]

Stewardship emphasis, however, has come to include not only the stewardship of money, but of time and talents as well. This extended emphasis has overlapped with new forms of stewardship training. Synodical leaders have been instructed so that they are able to give leadership training to women in congregational organizations. A facet of this training has been increased participation of synodical leaders in national workshops sponsored by the auxiliary. Another expression of this leadership has been the cooperation between the synod and the women's organizations, especially as LCW board members serve as observers to all major synodical committees.

The South Carolina Unit has sent delegates to each of the Triennial Conventions of Lutheran Church Women. At the first such meeting in 1965, Mrs. Herman Cauble was elected to a three-year term on the Board of Directors. Mrs. Harry Crout and Mrs. James B. Shealy have also served on that Board from South Carolina. In addition to these ladies, a number of SCLCW members have served on various committees for the auxiliary.

In 1981, the historical records of women's work in South Carolina were deposited in the archives of Dacus Library on the campus of Winthrop College in Rock Hill.[3] At the time an historian was appointed to collect historical items and deposit them with the library at ten-year intervals. Although records are cared for by Dacus Library, the agreement between Winthrop College and SCLCW stated that they remain the property of SCLCW.

During these years as South Carolina Lutheran Church Women, the organization has been blessed with outstanding Christian leadership. Local leaders, district assembly leaders, unit officers and board members have all combined with the membership to make the women's auxiliary of the South Carolina Lutheran Synod live up to its purpose ". . . to be a community of women which, in response to the Holy Spirit, engages in the mission of proclamation and reconciliation through its life and work and through the life and work of the LCA." At the close of these twenty-five years as Lutheran Church Women, there are 149 active organizations in the 160 congregations of synod with a total membership of over 6,200 women.[4] Growth during these years has been slow but steady. In 1987, instead of having the unit (synodical) convention, which had been held each year at

LCW officers: Gloria Rast, President; Betty Bradley, Vice-President; Linda Summers, Secretary; and Carolyn Torrence, Treasurer.

Newberry College with delegates from each congregational organization, an LCW Rally was held at the Radisson Hotel on May 23, to which all South Carolina Lutheran Church Women were invited and at which there was a pageant depicting the history of the SCLCW.[5] Later in the summer a constituting convention was held as a first step in the organizing of the new women's auxiliary. The SCLCW now is ready to take part in a new organization of women as Lutherans in America take another step in becoming "One" in the Lord's work.

PRESIDENTS OF LUTHERAN CHURCH WOMEN

1971-1973 .... Mrs. J. Harry Crout
1973-1975 .... Mrs. James B. Shealy
1975-1979 .... Mrs. D. Murray Shull, Jr.
1979-1981 .... Mrs. Thomas R. Peacock
1981-1983 .... Mrs. Wilbur Shealy
1983-1985 .... Mrs. Charles B. Shealy
1985-1987 .... Mrs. Heber Rast

Lutheran Church Youth

From 1968 to 1978, there was no synodical youth organization as such, but many youth were involved in the life and ministry of the church through the efforts of the synodical Youth Ministry Committee. Youth were asked to serve on LCA boards, synodical committees, congregational committees, and church councils. They assumed responsible roles in local congregations and were elected as delegates to LCA conventions.

The Rev. Lloyd W. Mitcham, Jr., who had been added to the synod staff in 1968 as Executive Secretary for Christian Education and Youth Ministry, played a vital role in the success of Youth Ministry in South Carolina, considered to be one of the most effective youth programs in the LCA. One of the weaknesses of youth ministry was the lack of an LCA or synodical organization; so Pastor Mitcham led the organization of the South Carolina program on a synod-committee/district-council arrangement. The synod committee was composed of one youth and one adult from each district; there was an equal number of adult and youth participants on the district youth councils. Members of the synod committee were included on the district councils, thus ideas were shared "through people, not paper."

Another weakness which was really felt by the congregational youth groups was the absence of any program materials from the LCA. Since this was a real difficulty for adult leaders, materials were prepared through the Synod office and distributed to the congregations. Adult Youth Ministry Conferences were also held at the beginning of the year from 1972-1977.

Beginning in 1974, there was a program sponsored by the LCA which gave impetus to Youth Ministry. Youth Staffers were sent into the synods,[6] each to work for one year. They were usually college students; some were taking a year out, and others were devoting their first year after graduation to church service. Thirteen young people served the synod as Youth Staffers.

Each year two district rallies were held. They focused on issues, projects, and worship. Among the programs enjoyed by the youth were an all-day sock hop, a Thanksgiving contemporary worship service, and a walk-a-thon to raise money for Meals-on-Wheels. Synodwide events also boosted the interest in congregational youth groups. These events took the form of both all-day mass rallies and smaller weekend retreats. One rally held at Newberry College featured districts challenging each other with whimsical contests based on the television show "Anything Goes." There were weekend retreats held at Camp Kinard for grades 7 through 9 and for grades 10 through 12. The activities of these conferences revolved around a theme, such as "New Religions," "God Don't Make No Junk," and "Death and Dying." There were also two-week camps at John's Island which involved the youth in migrant ministry.

One youth project in the early 1970's was raising money for a swimming pool at Camp Kinard.[7] It was dedicated on September 8, 1974. Beginning in 1972 and continuing to the present, youth have worked with the camp for Mentally Retarded at Camp Kinard. There are two one-week sessions where the youth work as counselors on a one-to-one basis, planning and leading activities ranging from Bible study to boat rides, from trips to the shopping malls to painting with pudding.

Governor Riley presents Youth Volunteer Award to LCY President, D'Etta Price.

From 1972 to 1978 the campers were clients from the Coastal Center, and in more recent years from the Midland's Center. From their experience as counselors at these camps, a number of youth have decided to go into careers in the field of special education therapy. In 1986, the LCY received the Governor's Youth Volunteer Award for its work with the MR camps.[8]

In 1974, memorials were presented at the LCA convention to re-establish a national youth organization, and the 1976

LCA convention voted to instruct the Division for Parish Services to assist synods that wished to develop their own youth organizations. Newberry District proposed a state youth organization for the South Carolina Synod, and in 1977 the synod convention adopted the proposal, the structure to be implemented by the synodical Youth Ministry Committee.[9]

First Lutheran Church Youth Officers: front row, Sara Moeller, President; Lori Shull, Secretary; and back row, Andy Massey, Vice-President; and John Greenwold, Treasurer.

Pastor Mitcham, Cindy Roof, Reedy Hopkins, Dottie Park, Sara Moeller, Jim Riser, Ginny Aull, Jenny Lanning, and Pastors Al Potter and Bob Coon began work immediately to put together a structure for the statewide youth organization.[10] By August 1978, Lutheran Church Youth (LCY) was ready to hold a constituting convention. One hundred and fifty delegates and twenty-nine staff members met at Newberry College August 3-5 to adopt a constitution and elect officers.[11] Congregational constitutions were to be based on the synod document.

The stated purpose was "to express their Christian faith in terms of worship, learning, witness, service, fellowship, and support ... develop leadership that is responsible and visible ... find a common identity as the younger members of the church, the Body of Christ." [12] For a congregational group to become an official member of the synod organization, it must "make a list of officers and enablers and make a pledge of financial support." Each district was required to have four elected officers and four adult enablers. The presidents of the district organizations were included on the Executive Board of the LCY, along with the synodical officers, to carry on business between annual conferences.

The new LCY worked closely with the synod Youth Ministry Committee, focusing on local youth groups and district assemblies, looking at broader ministries where youth could develop leadership, involve themselves in the life of the church, sponsor service projects, and cooperate with the LCA Division for Parish Services. LCY continued the MR camps, made PAL kits for migrant workers, carried out programs at the Lowman Home and Franke Home, and held leadership conferences. Annual convention/conferences were held to conduct the business of the organization as well as to provide new ideas for the congregational organizations and fellowship for the youth.

South Carolina youth have also participated in events which have brought them in contact with other synods of the LCA. In 1981, there was an international youth gathering at Purdue University; another was held in 1985; and regional events were held in 1980 at Furman University, in 1983 and 1986. South Carolina youth also took part in the Global Mission event in 1982 at Wittenberg University.

In 1985, the Rev. Robert L. Dasher was called as assistant to the Bishop upon the resignation of Pastor Mitcham. His work included responsibility for the Youth Ministry program. On July 27, 1987, LCY observed its tenth anniversary at Newberry College with the theme "Reaching Back, Looking Forward." [13] In 1987, Mrs. Nancy Padgett was hired on a part-time basis as the synod's youth ministry coordinator. (See page 51.)

PRESIDENTS OF THE LUTHERAN CHURCH YOUTH

1978-79	Sara Moeller
1979-80	Debbie Haigler
1980-81	Teresa Martin
1981-82	Donna Haigler
1982-83	Eric Wells
1983-84	Catherine Ficken
1984-85	Bryan Counts
1985-86	D'Etta Price
1986-87	Tom Henderson
1987-88	Derek Counts

Lutheran Men

Making gifts and loans to mission congregations continued to be the primary purpose of the Lutheran Men. In 1963, the Loan and Gift Fund was divided into two separate funds, the Mission Gift Fund and the Lutheran Men Loan Fund. In 1971, the goal for the Mission Gift Fund was raised from $7,500 to $12,000, and by 1987 had increased to $15,000. From 1971 to 1987, the Lutheran Men gave 26 different mission congregations over $233,000. These gifts were:

1971 $12,000 Redeemer, Greer ($5,000); Our Shepherd, Hartsville ($2,000); Trinity, Columbia ($2,000); St. Paul, Gaffney ($1,000); Augsburg, Union ($1,000); St. John, Beaufort ($500); and Holy Cross, Charleston ($500).

1972 $12,000 Trinity, Georgetown ($3,000); St. Paul, Gaffney ($3,000); Augsburg, Union ($3,000); Redeemer, Greer ($1,500); Our Shepherd, Hartsville ($1,000); and Holy Cross, Charleston ($500).

1973 $12,000 Trinity, Columbia ($3,000); Augsburg, Union ($3,000); St. Matthias, Easley ($1,000); Christ, Hilton Head ($1,000); St. Mark, Sullivan's Island ($1,000); Redeemer, Greer ($1,000), St. Paul, Gaffney ($1,000); Holy Cross, Charleston ($500); and Our Shepherd, Hartsville ($500).

1974 $12,000 Trinity, Columbia ($2,000); Augsburg, Union ($2,000); St. Paul, Gaffney ($2,000); Peace, Ladson ($1,000); Redeemer, Greer ($1,000); St. Mark, Isle of Palms ($1,000); Christ, Hilton Head ($1,000); St. Matthias, Easley ($1,000); Our Shepherd, Hartsville ($500); Holy Cross, Charleston ($500).

1975 $12,000 St. Mark, Isle of Palms ($4,000); St. Paul, Gaffney ($3,000); Redeemer, Greer ($2,000); St. Matthias, Easley ($1,500); Christ, Hilton Head ($1,500).

1976 $12,000 St. Paul, Gaffney ($4,000); Redeemer, Greer ($3,000); Christ, Hilton Head ($2,000); St. Mark, Isle of Palms ($1,500); St. Matthias, Easley ($1,500).

1977 $13,000 Peace, Ladson ($4,334); All Saints, Mt. Pleasant ($3,250); St. Matthias, Easley ($2,166); Christ, Hilton Head ($1,625); Redeemer, Greer ($1,625).

1978 $12,000 All Saints, Mt. Pleasant ($4,000); Peace, Ladson ($3,000); St. Matthias, Easley ($2,000); Shepherd of the Sea, Garden City ($1,500); King of Glory, North Myrtle Beach ($1,500).

1979 $13,000 Shepherd of the Sea ($5,000); All Saints, Mt. Pleasant ($3,000); King of Glory, North Myrtle Beach ($2,000); Peace, Ladson ($1,500); St. Matthias, Easley ($1,500).

1980 $14,000 King of Glory, North Myrtle Beach ($5,384.60); Shepherd of the Sea, Garden City ($3,230.80); All Saints, Mt. Pleasant ($2,153.80); Lord of Life, Harbison ($1,615.40); A Mighty Fortress, Sangaree ($1,615.40).

1981 $14,000 A Mighty Fortress, Sangaree ($5,384.40); King of Glory, North Myrtle Beach ($3,231.20); St. Matthias, Easley ($2,153.20); Lord of Life, Harbison ($1,615.60); All Saints, Mt. Pleasant ($1,615.60).

1982 $13,000 Cross and Crown, Florence ($5,000); A Mighty Fortress, Sangaree ($3,000); Lord of Life, Harbison ($2,000); All Saints, Mt. Pleasant ($1,500); St. Matthias, Easley ($1,500).

1983 $14,000 A Mighty Fortress, Sangaree ($3,230); King of Glory, North Myrtle Beach ($3,230); All Saints, Mt. Pleasant ($3,230); St. Peter, Pawleys Island ($2,155); Cross and Crown, Florence ($2,155).

1984 $15,000 Augsburg, Union ($3,462); St. Mark, Isle of Palms ($3,462); St. Peter, Pawleys Island ($3,462); Abiding Presence, York (2,307); Our Shepherd, Hartsville ($2,307).

LM Treasurer presents Mission Gift Fund checks to representatives of Augsburg, Union; St. Mark, Isle of Palms; St. Peter, Litchfield Beach; Abiding Presence, York; and Our Shepherd, Hartsville.

1985 $17,000 Cross and Crown, Florence ($3,966.67); St. Peter, Pawleys Island ($3,966.67); Christ the Servant, Conway ($3,966.67); Christus Victor, Columbia ($2,550); Ministry with the Deaf, Columbia (2,550).

1986 $17,500 A Mighty Fortress, Summerville ($4,083); Christus Victor, Columbia ($4,083); Our Shepherd, Hartsville ($4,083); St. Peter, Pawleys Island ($2,625); and Ministry with the Deaf, Columbia ($2,625).

1987 $19,000 Cross and Crown, Florence ($3,750); St. Peter, Pawleys Island ($3,750); Abiding Presence, York ($3,750); St. Mark, Blythewood ($3,750); Ministry with the Deaf, Columbia ($1,000); Living Springs, Columbia ($1,000); Christ the Servant, Conway ($1,000); Christ the King, Greenville ($500); Lake Wylie, Fort Mill ($500).[14]

From 1968 until 1976, the Honorary Life and Memorial Membership fee was the only designated money for the Lutheran Men's Loan Fund. Since 1968 over 1,250 Honorary Life and over 300 Memorial memberships have been received for the Loan Fund. This fund also received a gift of $40,557.09 through the will of a Lutheran layman, Mr. Walter Henry Proescholdt.[15] In 1976, the Committee of One Hundred was established to encourage at least 100 men of the synod to give $100 each to the Loan Fund every year. The Loan Fund has assets of $726,171.63[16] with a goal of $1,000,000. There are 12 churches with loans in the amount of $200,539.55,[17] and since 1971, 19 churches have received loans totalling over $777,000.[18]

In 1966, the Lutheran Men began thinking about building a retreat center. They appointed a committee and were hard at work when the synod decided to develop a Camp and Conference Center. During the year 1970-71, Camp Kinard was constructed, and in 1970 the Lutheran Men constructed the first cottage at Camp Kinard. They also constructed an additional lake and raised the dam of the existing lake by four feet. The mortgage on the cottage was burned at the State LM Convention in 1973. The Lutheran Men also spearheaded the construction of a shelter for the camp, and since the opening of the camp, have used its facilities regularly for retreats. In 1980, Lutheran Men adopted a $20,000 project for paving, sidewalks, landscaping, and a sprinkler system at the Coastal Retreat Center. By 1983, the funds were in hand, and the project was completed.

The Rev. James Fox addresses an LM Breakfast at synod convention.

Throughout the synod, the fourth Sunday in September is observed as Lutheran Men Sunday. At this time, all members of the congregations are encouraged to support the mission work of Lutheran Men. The synod organization has provided many programs, films, and cassette tapes for the local units to use. It has also published a regular newsletter, "The Epistle," to keep congregational units informed about the happenings of Lutheran Men. An annual convention in the fall provides men with the opportunity to review the work of the synodical LM organization, elect officers, conduct other business, and present the annual gifts to mission congregations. Since 1979, a special LM award has been given to men who have served their synod, their congregation, and the auxiliary in an exemplary manner. No more than two awards are made each year. Recipients of the awards have been:

1979	Roy Seay
	Dr. Herman W. Cauble
1980	Harry Stoudenmire
	Raymond S. Caughman
1981	Howard Cook, Jr.
	Dr. Karl W. Kinard
1982	Jim Brittingham
	Reid Wingard
1983	James Hallman
	Phillip T. Kelly, Jr.
1984	Dr. Fred E. Dufford
	B. O. Derrick

LM officers are installed (left to right): Keith Hutto, president; the Rev. Gene Beck (hidden), pastoral advisor; Wayne Caughman, treasurer; Heber Rast, vice-president; Miller Shealy, secretary; Wayne Sease, promotional secretary; by previous pastoral advisor, the Rev. Olin Chassereau.

1985	W. Archie Dodgen
	The Rev. John Koch
1986	Cecil H. Bowers
	The Rev. Charles E. Bernhardt
1987	Raymond Boozer
	The Rev. Dr. James S. Aull[19]

Through the years the Lutheran Men have had excellent leadership from their officers and members. Presidents of the Lutheran Men since 1971 have been:

1971-2	Raymond S. Caughman
1973-4	Reid S. Wingard
1975	Robert N. Hubbs
1976	Louis H. Martens, Jr.
1977	Lawrence D. Chapman
1978	R. Paul Richardson
1979	William B. Drake
1980	Carol O. Ulmer
1981-2	James N. Hallman
1983	Larry Kyzer
1984	Keith Hutto
1985	Heber Rast, Jr.
1986	Miller W. Shealy, Sr.
1987	Wayne E. Caughman

Chapter Four—Institutions and Agencies

The institutions of the synod provide great opportunities for unique ministry programs not only for Lutherans, but all people of the state. From camping, to college and seminary education, to a home for the aged and infirm, the South Carolina Synod has provided financial and volunteer support for these institutions, which in turn fulfill many ministry goals of the synod.

Lowman Home

By 1970, the Lowman Home had served the people of South Carolina in a very special ministry for sixty years. Having received an estate consisting of over 950 acres of land and some money, Lowman Home was established by the synod for the care of the aged and helpless.[1] The 1970's brought new leadership to the Board of Trustees when Mr. Deems Haltiwanger became chairman in 1970, only the fourth person to hold that position. He served until 1972, when Dr. Robert L. Hock was elected chairman. Elected in May 1972, Dr. Hock had to resign in October 1972, when he accepted a call to the Florida Synod. Dr. William F. Austin succeeded Dr. Hock and continues to serve as Chairman of the Board.

Under the leadership of the Rev. Dr. J. Kenneth Webb as President, the Lowman Home, with the infirmary, changed from a home for the aged to a geriatric center, beginning in 1964. The home was fully accredited and appropriately licensed to provide all three levels of nursing care—residential, intermediate, and skilled nursing, including Medicare. A fourth level of care, self-sustaining residency, was later added. The home has been and continues to be open to any person who is over 18 years of age and needs the services offered by Lowman Home.

Skilled nursing care is for those guests who need total or considerable nursing care during the entire day, including those who may be bedridden or up part of the day in a

68

Lowman Home President, Dr. Kenneth Webb.

wheel-chair. Intermediate care is for guests who are able to be up and around their rooms and can care for their daily personal hygiene, but who need some assistance with walking and may require assistance with dressing and bathing. Boarding-home guests are capable of caring for themselves, walking the covered walkways without assistance to the central dining area and requiring only a small amount of supervision. The self-sustaining residents are those who live in either a cottage or an efficiency apartment located on Lowman Home grounds. These residents are at least 62 years old and can sustain themselves under normal living conditions.

The 1970's brought changes and opportunities to the Lowman Home. For instance, on July 1, 1974, the Southeastern Synod withdrew from the ownership and operation of Lowman Home, making it the sole property and responsibility of the South Carolina Synod.[2] Also, in that same year, four cottages were completed, bringing the number of units in the self-sustaining residency program to 21.

In October 1975, the Home completed a new 29-bed addition to the Boliek Infirmary at a cost of $840,000 financed again by gifts and bequests plus a Hill-Burton grant. This addition, known as Memorial Wing, brought the number of beds in the Boliek Infirmary to 85.[3]

Later, in 1977, the Bernice H. Moose Activities Center was dedicated with no debt on the $90,000 building.[4] With its completion, the Home's physical plant topped the $4.5 million mark.

An important event for Lowman Home took place in 1978 when the Wynne C. Boliek Infirmary was approved as a

The Activities Center building.

dually certified facility by the State Board of Health, making it possible for all beds to be used interchangeably for either skilled nursing or intermediate care.[5] The Lowman Home family also grew. The staff included 155 employees, and there were well over 200 guests.

The Home's friends have also increased in number over the years. Volunteer groups have come to the Home regularly to work, to entertain, or merely to visit with guests. Additionally, there has been a long list of business and professional people who have shared their time and talents toward the ongoing of Lowman Home. Church groups throughout the South and particularly in South Carolina have played a major part in helping make Lowman Home what it is today, a leader in the nursing home field with a caring heart.

In order for the members of the South Carolina Synod to have one of the finest total-care nursing centers of its kind anywhere, the Home's trustees, administration, and staff have always been alert to improving the facility. In August 1981, the Deems Haltiwanger Building was dedicated. The building at completion cost $1,543,125, and it provided 40 private rooms with private baths as a unit in the Residential Care (Boarding Home) section.[6]

Lowman Home depends on others' benevolence in many

The Haltiwanger building.

ways. The quality of life of Lowman Home guests has been enhanced from the very beginning with the volunteers. In 1981, nearly 500 volunteers gave unselfishly of themselves to the Home and its guests. Visiting, sewing, luncheons, trips and help from loving volunteers have made life much better for guests since the early days. Christmas at Lowman Home that year (1981) was blessed with 175 groups assisting with gifts for the residents.

As the Home progressed into the 1980's, many good things continued to happen, but the burden of economic restraints in the area of indigent care began to be felt. Shrinking federal money placed a hardship on Lowman Home's activities. Indigent-care guests were subsidized by nearly $500,000 in 1983 from the Home's reserves.[7] Some of this subsidy was offset by contributions from the synods, individuals, and churches, but the Home had to bear over $240,000 that year. The synod's budgeted support for the Home has grown from $49,000 in 1981 to $100,000 in 1987.[8] During this time the funds from the Home's Mother's Day Appeal and generous gifts at Christmas and during other times of the year have reduced the shortfall caused by indigent care.

In January of 1984, the Board of Trustees was forced to take a dramatic step in an effort to reduce the rising indigent-care costs. The Home's admission policies were amended so that for each three guests admitted to the Home, two have to demonstrate the ability to pay the full rate, until the roster of indigent-care recipients does not exceed one-third of the available beds or available space, or until the Indigent-Care Fund exceeds the cost of one-third of available beds or space. This action was necessary to insure the continued operation of the Home. Moreover, the Indigent-Care Fund mentioned above was established and comprised of synodical apportionment, one-half of the investment income from the Houck Trusts and all other contributions specifically designated for indigent care.[9]

Along with the problem of indigent care, the 1980's have brought blessings, also. Services to the Home and to the community have been expanded with the Education and Training Center under the direction of Dr. J. Obert Kempson. The center has provided a learning setting for student nurses at the University of South Carolina, students in the licensed practical nursing program at Baptist Medical Center, and Master's Degree Candidates in Social Work at USC. Also, Lutheran Theological Southern Seminary and Newberry College students come to the Home to learn through the Education and Training Center. In 1986, the Home expanded its caring hands to the operation of an adult day-

Residents participate in an exercise program at Lowman Home.

care center in Columbia in leased space at Ebenezer Lutheran Church. If this pilot project is successful, the Home plans to investigate further expansion in other areas.

Earlier Mrs. Bessie Black and her daughter, Sara, made a substantial contribution to the Home. In 1983, Lowman Home again received a gift in the form of revenue from a trust fund valued at $369,912 from Miss Sara Black.[10]

Lowman Home received one of its larger gifts, $1,128,163, from the estate of Mrs. Fannie A. Roesel of Augusta, Georgia. The gift is to be paid in increments over a 25-year period. Lowman Home has received special gifts amounting to millions of dollars over her 75-year history.[11] A bequest from the estate of Herman Langford in Newberry was made in 1986.

The year 1986 marked a significant time in the Lowman Home's life, seventy-five years of service to God and to a special segment of His people. As its gift of celebration, the Home refurbished the Wynne C. Boliek Infirmary.[12] A Service of Celebration and Thanksgiving with over 450 people in attendance was held on September 21, 1986, at St. Thomas, Chapin, followed by a reception in the Home's Activities Center. Visitors were also invited to view the refurbished and renovated infirmary. The $75,000 goal as an anniversary offering for the Indigent-Care Fund was exceeded.[13]

Newly elected Lowman Home President, the Rev. Boyd F. Cook.

Another Home anniversary was celebrated in 1986. Dr. Webb celebrated his 25th anniversary as President of the Lowman Home. He was honored in the celebration service, and the Home's annual Employee Appreciation Day was named for him in honor of his 25 years of service.[14]

Dr. Webb retired in 1987, and he was honored with a retirement dinner in Columbia where over 400 people enjoyed the "roasting" and "toasting" of Dr. Webb and his wife. The Rev. Boyd F. Cook, a member of the Board of Trustees, was elected President.[15]

Lowman Home is operated in 1987, just as it was founded seventy-five years ago, on the strong belief in and reliance upon the benevolence of God's people. Although run by the South Carolina Synod, Lowman Home's 1986-87 budget of $4.8 million is not totally contributed by the synod. Rather, the Home's operation is the result of seventy-five years of gifts, both big and small, from hundreds of caring people who see the need for the services of Lowman Home and have a strong faith in the Home to provide those services in the name of God.

Lutheran Theological Southern Seminary

During the past seventeen years, Southern Seminary has experienced steady growth and has faced significant challenges. It has seen an increase in enrollment and in numbers of faculty and staff. Its budget has risen from $340,000 to $1.8 million. It has been through two changes of curriculum and adjustments in degree programs. It has added a major building in its award-winning Lineberger Library and has undertaken extensive renovations and improvements on other facilities. Its community has become more diverse, more inclusive, and more ecumenical. It has prepared itself to enter the Evangelical Lutheran Church in America, facing new opportunities and offering leadership. These years—in the midst of which the Seminary celebrated its sesquicentennial year—have been marked both by a certain maturity as an academic institution and as a community of faith and by an engagement with new realities, new possibilities for ministry.

When Hugh George Anderson became president of the seminary in the fall of 1970, the institution was poised for an era of energy and progress.[16] In many ways, the administration of F. Eppling Reinartz had stabilized the seminary for such an advance: at the end of his tenure, Dr. Reinartz had worked with the Board of Trustees on a planning proj-

The Lineberger Memorial Library at LTSS.

ect entitled "The Next Phase of This Seminary's Development." [17] Those plans would begin to take shape early in the 1970's under the seminary's new president. Respected as a teacher by a generation of students, widely known as a speaker and preacher, Dr. Anderson brought to his office a vision of academic development and a commitment to service of the church.

Central to the changes that would occur was the cultivation of financial resources. The Outreach Appeal, a major effort to build endowment, was initiated in 1972 and eventually drew over $2.7 million in gifts.[18] The Rev. Curtis E. Derrick was called to assist Dr. Kenneth Hewitt with this appeal and then was named full-time Director of Development upon Dr. Hewitt's retirement in 1973.[19] This campaign would lead to the first endowed chair, the Dewey F. Beam Professorship of Pastoral Care, to the renovation of three buildings, to expanded programs in continuing education, to student scholarships, and to the endowment fund passing the half-million dollar mark.[20] The creation of the Columbia Advisory Council would bring additional local support to the work of the seminary.[21] By the middle of the decade major grants had been received from the Cannon Trust and the Cannon Foundation, from the Lilly Foundation, and from the Lineberger Foundation. Throughout the seventeen-year period, two benevolent insurance companies, Aid Association for Lutherans and Lutheran Brotherhood, provided annual support for continuing education, student aid, and faculty development.[22]

Early in the new administration adjustments were made in the areas of the president's responsibility: new staff configurations added flexibility and broadened resources to the school's leadership. The strengthening of the development office, of course, would aid the president in his fund-raising efforts. To provide assistance with both business and academic matters, James S. Aull, Professor of Old Testament since 1962, became the Administrative Assistant to the President.[23] In order to extend its programs for pastors, other church workers and members of congregations, the seminary in 1972 called a Director of Continuing Education, the Rev. Martin F. Saarinen, who in addition to creating and guiding continuing education events would develop, by 1974, the Doctor of Ministry degree program.[24] With the calling of Robert C. Schultz as Director of Internship and Professor of Pastoral Care a full administrative team was in place by the fall of 1975.[25]

The heart of the seminary's task remained the preparation of people for ministries in the church. A new curriculum, initiated in 1974, gave students a larger role in the shaping of their own education: the core of required courses was reduced and more elective hours became possible.[26] The Master of Religious Education degree became the Master of Arts in Religion in 1973, also reflecting a broadening of concept and an additional freedom for the student to shape a program suited to his or her professional needs.[27] An evaluation by the American Association of Theological Schools was conducted in 1972; Southern Seminary again received accreditation and remained the only accredited theological school in South Carolina.[28] Within the academic program, opportunities were expanding. More serious attention was given to the presence of Methodist students on the campus, and negotiations began with the United Methodist Church in the hope of adding an adjunct professor with responsibility for courses in Methodist polity, history and theology.[29] The first woman with a Master of Divinity degree graduated in 1974;[30] there would be increasing numbers of women in the student population in all degree programs. Following a trend in other theological schools and with encouragement from the professional leadership committees of the supporting synods, the seminary in 1976 began granting credit for Clinical Pastoral Education.[31] A gift from anonymous donors in North Carolina established an endowed lectureship in memory of Jacob L. Morgan, former president of the North Carolina Synod. As a result of this gift, distinguished theologians would add another dimension to the academic program for the seminary community and for pastors and church members in the area.[32]

In the second half of President Anderson's term, there were significant developments within the Board of Trustees and among the faculty. A series of Trustee Development seminars, supported by the Lilly Endowment, brought deeper levels of involvement among the Trustees and fostered a new relationship between Trustees, faculty and administration.[33] One such meeting led to the reformulation of the seminary's statement of purpose, a statement thought through and written by faculty and trustees and signaling a sense of partnership in the mission of the seminary.

> The purpose of Lutheran Theological Southern Seminary is to educate men and women for the church's ministry, primarily in the Lutheran Church in America, including theological preparation for ordained and lay ministry and continuing theological education of laity and clergy. This theological education seeks to be evangelical in content, relevant to contemporary society, and ecumenical in scope with the intent of developing persons to become spiritually mature, theologically competent, and ethically sensitive within an inclusive and caring community.[34]

New faculty appointments were made necessary by the resignation of men who had played prominent roles in the seminary's life over many years: Arnold E. Carlson in Contemporary Theology, Gordon A. Beaver in Church Music, Richard M. Bland in Old Testament, James S. Aull in Old Testament, George Frederick Schott in Systematic Theology and J. Obert Kempson in Pastoral Care.[35]

One new faculty position in the field of New Testament was created during this time and was filled by Charles P. Sigel.[36] Other faculty members to join the staff during the Anderson administration were Scott H. Hendrix in Church History, Carl F. W. Ficken in Theology and Culture, L. David Miller in Church Music, Michael J. Root in Systematic Theology, and Robert J. Marshall in Old Testament.[37] Mack C. Branham, Jr., became adminstrative assistant and registrar following the resignation of Professor Aull in 1979.[38] In the midst of these changes in its composition, the faculty was also coming to a different stance within the institution. This occurred in its relationship to the Board of Trustees, through the opportunities offered by the Trustee Development seminars, and in having a representative attend Board meetings beginning in 1974.[39] The faculty also prepared a faculty handbook, accepted a larger function in the search for new faculty members and in its own governance, and began participation in an enriched sabbatical program.[40] A curriculum review process which began in 1976 involved the faculty in examination of the objectives for the seminary's educational tasks and of the expectations for its graduates.[41]

With the completion of the Lineberger Library in 1975, the physical plant of the campus seemed adequate for the seminary's program. What had to be done next was to maintain and improve the existing buildings. Extensive and long-needed renovation was begun for the dormitory, the Voigt classroom building, and the Price House which had formerly housed the library.[42] The oldest structure on campus was renovated and named the Beam Dormitory following a substantial gift by Dewey F. Beam of Cherryville, North Carolina.[43] A major landscaping project was carried out in 1976. Needlepoint cushions were provided for the chapel's altar rail under the leadership of Sunny Anderson, wife of the president, through the artistic design of student Michael Knudson, and by the hand work of people in the supporting synods.[44] The undercroft of Christ Chapel was renamed Reinartz Hall in 1978 following the death of former president F. Eppling Reinartz.[45]

By the end of President Anderson's term in 1981, Southern Seminary had experienced a decade of growth and change. Largely through the addition of the Doctor of Ministry program, the student enrollment had increased from 120 to 160; over 750 persons were served in continuing education.[46] The budget passed the one million dollar mark. The library was housed in an exciting new building and had grown to 74,000 volumes.[47] At the time of its one hundred and fiftieth anniversary, the seminary seemed to have reached one of its healthiest moments. A new 16mm film, "So Send I You," was circulating throughout the Southeast, giving to congregations the picture of a modern campus and a vibrant community.[48] As part of the sesquicentennial celebration, lectures were presented on the school's history: each lecture was given on one of the former locations of the seminary and thus brought together analysis of the school's past and recollection and acknowledgment of other places of importance to the life of the institution.

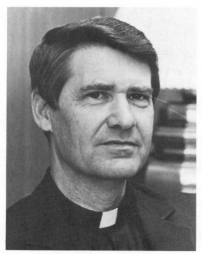

LTSS President, Dr. Mack C. Branham.

Upon the resignation of Dr. Anderson to become president of Luther College in Decorah, Iowa, the Board of Trustees appointed a search committee and named Mack C. Branham to serve as Acting President, effective in January of 1982.[49] The search committee worked for a year before choosing a person already involved in the school's leadership.[50] A native of Columbia and a graduate of Southern, Dr. Branham held a doctorate in Education, Administration and Communication and was familiar with the business operation of the seminary. At a time when the costs of theological education were rising dramatically and when student enrollment seemed about to decline, the Board found a person close at hand who could lead the seminary through what were perceived to be some difficult years ahead. The Inauguration was held on January 28, 1983, with Bishop James Crumley as preacher.[51] The Seminary under Dr. Branham's leadership prepared to face the challenges and opportunities of the 1980's.

With a new president, once again adjustments in administrative responsibilities were desirable. A business manager and registrar was hired in 1982; and three years later, the registrar's duties were moved to another office.[52] By 1984, for the first time in nearly forty years, the Seminary returned to the pattern of president-and-dean: Paul T. Jersild, formerly dean at Wartburg Seminary, assumed the position of academic dean and was named also Professor of Theology and Ethics.[53] Relieved of primary tasks in both the business and academic operations, President Branham was free to play a larger role in institutional development. The sudden death of Dr. Curtis Derrick in February of 1985 was a serious blow to the seminary.[54] Dr. Derrick's many friendships in the Southeast, his deep spirituality and his intense commitment to Southern Seminary had been one of the school's great strengths. During his thirteen years in the development office, the endowment had grown from $338,000 to almost $4 million.[55] By the fall of 1985, a new development officer, Dr. Clyde Kaminska, had begun his work, and within the next two years, he would be assisted by Pastor John Largen, who held responsibility for church relations and student recruitment, and by Ellen Stallworth, who managed media relations.[56] The presence of these two full-time additional staff members marked a commitment by the Board of Trustees to the whole development program of the seminary. Thus in 1987, Dr. Branham headed an administrative team which included an enlarged development staff, an academic dean, a registrar, and a business manager.

Early in Dr. Branham's administration, several major gifts to the seminary were to have a significant impact on the future direction of the institution. One of these gifts was the new Flentrop Organ for Christ Chapel.[57] Long a dream of the seminary, the organ became a reality through the generosity of Anna Barbara Fisher of Winston-Salem,

North Carolina, and her mother, Mrs. Loula Schaeffer Fisher of Concord, North Carolina. Presented in memory of Miss Fisher's father, the Arthur William Fisher Memorial Organ was dedicated on Reformation Day 1985. Additional gifts by Miss Fisher provided for maintenance of the organ, recitals, and music and worship workshops. The second gift came to establish the Lineberger Library Endowment Fund, a continuation of the long-time support of the seminary and especially its library by J. Harold Lineberger.[58] The third gift, considered at the time to be the largest single gift by an individual donor, was received in the fall of 1984 from Seminary Trustee and Atlanta, Georgia executive, Richard C. Kessler.[59] The designation of this gift would be determined after study of the seminary's needs. In addition to these large contributions, hundreds of individuals across the country contributed to the school's second endowed professorship: initiated in 1980, the campaign to fund a Hugh George Anderson Chair exceeded its goal of $300,000 in November of 1982 and was designated by the Board as the Chair in Church History.[60] In 1981, the North Carolina Synod had begun designating monies from its Michael Peeler Endowment for the eventual establishment of another endowed professorship; throughout the 1980's, the synod continued to make annual gifts from the Peeler Funds, aiming toward $250,000 in accumulated contributions—with earnings, a $300,000 endowment.[61]

Following Mr. Kessler's gift, the Board established a Long-Range Planning Committee which would draw on the expertise of people in varied fields across the Southeast in order to evaluate key areas of the seminary's program and to make recommendations to the Board about the future of the school.[62] The whole committee of some thirty-five people met with the Board and faculty in August of 1985; then, working in subcommittees over the next nine months, they prepared a report entitled *Vision 21* for consideration by the Board.[63] Numerous recommendations would be acted on by appropriate committees in the following months. One of the major recommendations—and the one responded to most quickly by the Board—had to do with the increased effort in the area of development: it was this action by the

Board that led to additional staffing in the development
office and an energetic program to raise funds, to extend
awareness of the school to potential students and benefactors, to enhance the seminary's image, and generally to
strengthen the institution for its missions in the church.

A significant issue explored during the period of this
long-range study was the question of location. Among the
task groups of the Long-Range Planning Committee, attention had been given to the values and liabilities of the Columbia campus and to the possible advantages of relocation
to another site, most notably Atlanta. As this conversation
was occurring within the seminary's own structures, the
Consultation on Theological Education of the Commission
on the New Lutheran Church was also re-evaluating the
location and mission of seminaries across the church: in its
final report, the Consultation advised that Southern Seminary study relocating in Atlanta.[65] Both the Consultation's
report and *Vision 21* thus had placed this issue before the
Board of Trustees in the spring of 1986; the Board agreed to
further study of the issue but asked that the committee
appointed for that study also consider other locations, and
that it examine the benefits of staying in Columbia.[66] When
that committee reported to the Board in October of 1986,
the Board reaffirmed its commitment to the Columbia location but agreed to give further consideration to the possible
establishment of a Lutheran House of Studies in Atlanta.[67]

Another major development during the middle of this
decade lay in the composition of the faculty. In 1985, Mary
B. Havens became an Assistant Professor of Church History and the first woman on the faculty; she replaced Scott
H. Hendrix.[68] In 1986, after seeing the seminary through
the dedication of the Fisher Organ, L. David Miller retired;
Robert D. Hawkins became Assistant Professor of Worship
and Music in the fall of 1986.[69] The 1986-1987 academic year
brought more changes. The Board called Daryl S. Everett to
become Dewey F. Beam Professor of Pastoral Care, and
Professor Austin F. Shell became Director of Contextual
Education which included supervision of the internship program.[70] Two professors also announced their retirement:
Harold F. Park, who had taught Christian Education and

Church Administration since 1961, and W. Richard Fritz, who had served as Librarian since 1947[71] and had seen the library's collection grow from 13,500 to 95,000 volumes.[72] In April 1987, the Board of Trustees named Luther E. Lindberg Professor of Educational Ministry and Mitzi Jarrett Derrick Director of the Library and Assistant Professor of Bibliography.[73] In the spring of 1987, Dr. Robert J. Marshall announced his retirement, and Dr. Lamontte M. Luker was called in October to be Assistant Professor of Old Testament. The seminary also announced that former Bishop of the Lutheran Church in America, James R. Cumley, Jr., would join the faculty and administration of the school as Distinguished Visiting Professor of Ecumenism.[74]

Through this period Southern's faculty persisted in providing leadership to the church, as authors, speakers, board members, and workshop leaders. In the summer of 1986, the faculty issued its first theological journal, TAP-ROOT, an annual publication by which seminary faculty, students and guest lecturers would present essays, sermons and book reviews to encourage reflection and conversation on the campus and in the church.[75]

In September 1987, Pope John Paul, II visited Columbia. In coordination with this visit, Southern Seminary, the LCA, and the National Conference of Catholic Bishops hosted a colloquy titled "Day of Dialogue" the day following the Pope's visit. Johannes Cardinal Willebrands, President of the Vatican Secretariat for Promoting Christian Unity, was the principal speaker, and LCA Bishop James R. Crumley gave the response. This event was attended by over 300 church leaders, pastors, and laity. Medals were struck for the event by the LCA and were given to the sponsors and to Cardinal Willebrands. Miniature medals were given to each person in attendance.[76]

The academic program of the seminary was also undergoing expansion. A new curriculum, introduced in 1982, placed more emphasis on a strong core of coursework and yet allowed opportunity for elective studies; the curriculum was clearly related to the expectations of the church for its ministers.[77] A perception was growing that Southern Seminary was becoming more demanding in its academic program. The program was reviewed again in the early 1980's and won accreditation from both the Association of Theological Schools and from the Southern Association of Colleges and Universities.[78] The internship program was widely recognized as one of the finest among Lutheran seminaries.[79] In 1982, the faculty approved an ambitious program designed to enable bivocational black pastors to receive a Master of Divinity degree over an expanded period of years as they continued their secular employment and their pastoral duties.[80] Other black students were enrolled in the regular Master of Divinity studies. A relationship with the Dominican Order brought Roman Catholic students into certain courses. The number of women students increased steadily, reaching a high of 50 in 1986, 29.6% of the student population.[81] More students entered the seminary after having worked in other careers and begun raising a family; the average age of seminarians rose, and diversity within the student community was a key characteristic and a stimulus for the whole campus. The seminary began offering off-campus opportunities through the Urban Training Organization of Atlanta, the Appalachian Ministries Educational Resource Center in Berea, Kentucky, and the National Capital Semester for Seminarians at Wesley Seminary as well as the Lutheran House of Studies, both in Washington, D. C.[82] New continuing education programs, such as the Summer Institute for Leadership in Ministry and the Academy of Bible and Theology, initiated in 1980 and 1986 respectively, provided varied schedules of courses for pastors and other church members.

Maintenance of the campus buildings became a major item on the school's agenda during the 1980's. Various types of improvement had to be undertaken for the president's home, for student apartments and for faculty housing; substantial grants from the Lineberger Foundation and the Cannon Trust as well as other gifts and grants made this work possible.[83] The chapel windows, which because of loosened and falling glass had for some years been of concern, evolved into a rather dangerous problem: the Board finally had to authorize replacement of the windows, and that work was carried out in the summer of 1987.[84] Rising costs,

Replacing the stained-glass windows in Christ Chapel, LTSS.

inflation, and the necessity of dealing with long-delayed maintenance problems forced the seminary for the first time in recent decades to operate at a deficit in the middle years of the 1980's and to borrow money for extensive projects such as the replacement of the chapel windows.[85] The increased efforts of the development office, a Columbia-area capital funds appeal under the sponsorship of the Columbia Advisory Council, and participation in the One in Mission campaign of the new Evangelical Lutheran Church in America were seen as avenues for a return to financial stability.

This history of Southern Seminary during the 1970's and 1980's is not complete without acknowledgement of the leadership and devotion of members of the Board of Trustees, Alumni/ae, Auxiliary members, and benefactors. The story of a theological school is a story of God's people exercising ministry; administrators, faculty, staff, students, trustees, constituents, benefactors. Students stand at the heart of the institution, engaged each year in reflection and in activities of both preparation and ministry. Those students become pastors and church workers, the new leaders of the church. It is no accident that Southern Seminary graduates have provided notable service to the church in the offices, for example, of Bishop of the Lutheran Church in America, James Crumley, or Editor of *The Lutheran,* Edgar Trexler;[86] nor is it accident that Southern Seminary graduates serve and are members of congregations, large and small, across the country and in Japan, New Guinea, India, Liberia, Namibia, Tanzania, Austria, England, and Germany. Such service is entirely consistent with the school's stated purpose. To make this ministry possible, many people must perform the often thankless tasks of seminary life. Devotion to the school and to their ministries is evident from the long tenure of members of the seminary's staff in all areas. Southern Seminary has come to be known as a community because of the people—students, staff, administrators, faculty, trustees, constituents, benefactors—who come together under the call and presence of God and who join in the proclamation of the Gospel.

Lutheridge

Located in Arden, North Carolina, Lutheridge celebrated its 25th anniversary of camping ministry for the Lutheran Church in 1975. Celebrations included an anniversary banquet, a special worship service, memorabilia display, and the renaming of Leadership Hall to Thornburg Hall, in honor of the Rev. Dr. J. Lewis Thornburg, the first Executive Director. A much-needed endowment fund was begun by a gift from the Lutheran Church of the Ascension, Savannah, Georgia.[87] Throughout the years, the camp's operations have been funded by contributions from the supporting synods and individuals and from campers' fees. Special camping appeals in each supporting synod allowed

Senior High Drama in Chapel at Lutheridge.

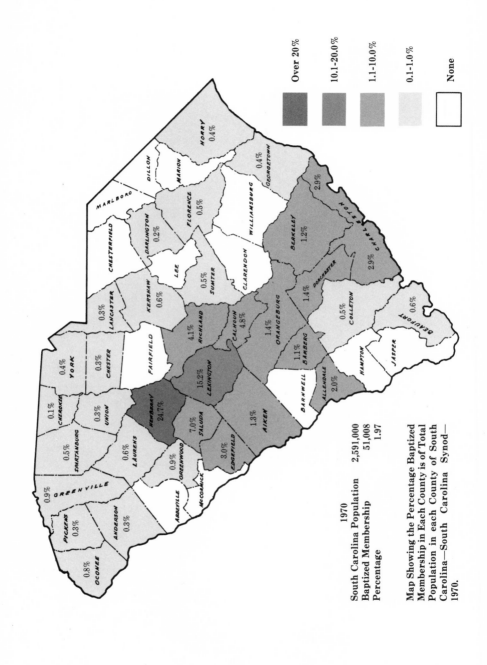

Over 20%

10.1–20.0%

1.1–10.0%

0.1–1.0%

None

1970
South Carolina Population   2,591,000
Baptized Membership   51,008
Percentage   1.97

Map Showing the Percentage Baptized
Membership in Each County is of Total
Population in each County of South
Carolina—South Carolina Synod—
1970.

HORRY 0.4%

DILLON

MARLBORO

MARION

GEORGETOWN 0.4%

CHARLESTON 2.9%

FLORENCE 0.5%

WILLIAMSBURG 0.4%

CHESTERFIELD

DARLINGTON 0.2%

BERKELEY 1.2%

LEE

CLARENDON

DORCHESTER 1.4%

KERSHAW 0.6%

SUMTER 0.5%

COLLETON 0.5%

LANCASTER 0.3%

ORANGEBURG 1.4%

BEAUFORT 0.6%

RICHLAND 4.1%

CALHOUN 4.8%

FAIRFIELD

BAMBERG 1.1%

JASPER

YORK 0.4%

CHESTER 0.3%

LEXINGTON 15.2%

HAMPTON

CHEROKEE 0.1%

UNION 0.3%

NEWBERRY 24.7%

SALUDA 7.0%

AIKEN 1.3%

BARNWELL

ALLENDALE 2.0%

SPARTANBURG 0.5%

LAURENS 0.6%

GREENWOOD 0.9%

EDGEFIELD 3.0%

GREENVILLE 0.9%

ABBEVILLE

McCORMICK

PICKENS 0.3%

ANDERSON 0.3%

OCONEE 0.8%